THE
GREATEST
STORY

THE DIVINE NARRATIVE OF REDEMPTION UNVEILED THROUGHOUT SCRIPTURE

Theodoros Kontopoulos

INTERNATIONAL
PETRADI
ΠΕΤΡΑΔΙ
PUBLISHING HOUSE

The Greatest Story: The Divine Narrative of Redemption Unveiled throughout Scripture

Original Greek Copyright © 2016 by Theodoros Kontopoulos
English translation © 2025 by Petradi International Publishing House, LLC
All rights reserved.

Petradi International Publishing House books may be purchased in bulk at special discounts for sales promotion, corporate gifts, ministry, fund-raising, or educational purposes. Special editions can also be created to specifications. For details, contact Special Sales Dept., Petradi International Publishing House at info@petradipublishing.com.

Visit our website at www.petradipublishing.com.

Library of Congress Control Number:
ISBN: 978-1-968609-00-9
eBook ISBN: 978-1-968609-01-6

Cover Design by Dan Pitts, Dan Pitts LLC
Interior design by Typewriter Creative Co.

Printed in India
TP
10 9 8 7 6 5 4 3 2 1

TABLE OF CONTENTS

PROLOGUE

OUR WORLD IS FILLED WITH CONTRADICTIONS AND DEAD ends. Countless times, life does not seem to make any sense. So, faced with this reality, many people conclude that true meaning does not exist, that everything happens by chance. They say: "Let us do the best we can in this meaningless world. Let's eat, drink, and be merry because tomorrow we die."

The world of the Bible confronts this misunderstanding of reality. It is only in the Bible where we can find the absolute truth about ourselves, the world we inhabit, and the One who gives purpose and meaning to everything. The Bible challenges everything we take for granted, as it invites us to see our life, human history, and the entire creation as parts of a great story; *the greatest story of all.*

If we choose to examine our world through the lens of God's revelation, we will discover marvelous light where we previously couldn't see anything but darkness. Surprised, we will realize that there is no such thing as luck; that human history doesn't move in aimless circles, but that everything has a specific purpose; that everything comes from the Lord Jesus Christ and exists for Him; and that it is the Lord who holds together all things and gives meaning to everything.

This realization helps us understand that we aren't the world's center. And that we aren't the Bible's center either. It is only then that we can read it correctly. The Bible doesn't primarily speak about us. *The Bible was given to us, but it doesn't speak first and foremost about us. The Bible's center is the Lord Jesus.*

The Bible is the testimony of God about His Son. Indeed, the Bible is the portrait of God the Son, the portrait which God the Father has painted through the Holy Spirit. The Bible is the God-breathed narration of the greatest story ever told, which has as its purpose the revelation and glorification of its perfect Hero, the Lord Jesus.

In this story, we see the Lord becoming the last Adam to succeed where the first had failed, as He crushed the ancient serpent's head on the cross while it wounded His heel.

We see the Good Shepherd choosing to pursue His lost sheep and lay down His life for them so that they may have life and have it abundantly. In truth, have life unending, as His sheep are eternally secure in His almighty nail-pierced hands.

We see the great king becoming the servant king, who sacrifices His life on behalf and in the place of His rebellious people.

Above all else, we see the great Warrior going through hellfire to save His beloved maiden from the most horrific of dangers. This is how He most emphatically reveals His incomprehensible love for the elect of His heart, His bride, the church.

Dear reader, perhaps you think this story seems too good to be true. That only fairy tales have such a happy ending. The truth is that this story is both "too good' *and* "true.' This happy ending is true because it was secured with the precious blood of the Lord, the blood of the crucified and risen Savior, the blood of the New Covenant.

Indeed, the Bible doesn't primarily speak *about* us, but it was given *to* us. It is God the Father's love letter to His children, with which He reveals to them the Son of His love. With this letter, He invites His children into the covenant of His grace and into the loving fellowship of the Trinity. With this letter, He preserves them on their pilgrimage toward the heavenly homeland. With this letter, He assures them of the imperishable, undefiled, and unfading inheritance that is kept in heaven for them.

Let us marvel at this great story through the pages of this book. Let us enjoy something of the indescribable beauty and greatness of its Hero. Let us find our place in this, the greatest story of all.

546. We know God only by Jesus Christ. Without this mediator all communion with God is taken away; through Jesus Christ we know God. All those who have claimed to know God, and to prove Him without Jesus Christ, have had only weak proofs. But in proof of Jesus Christ we have the prophecies, which are solid and palpable proofs. And these prophecies, being accomplished and proved true by the event, mark the certainty of these truths, and therefore the divinity of Christ. In Him then, and through Him, we know God.

547. Not only do we know God by Jesus Christ alone, but we know ourselves only by Jesus Christ. We know life and death only through Jesus Christ. Apart from Jesus Christ, we do not know what is our life, nor our death, nor God, nor ourselves. Thus without the Scripture, which has Jesus Christ alone for its object, we know nothing, and see only darkness and confusion in the nature of God, and in our own nature.

Blaise Pascal
Pensées, 546-547 (first edition: 1670 AD)

Thus, all of Scripture, as already said, is pure Christ, God's and Mary's Son. Everything is focused on this Son, so that we might know Him distinctively and in that way see the Father and the Holy Spirit eternally as one God. To him who has the Son, scripture is an open book; and the stronger his faith in Christ becomes, the more brightly will the light of Scripture shine for him.

Martin Luther
Treatise on the Last Words of David (1543 AD), LW 15:339

THE GREATEST STORY: INTRODUCTION

EVERYONE ENJOYS A GOOD STORY. ONE OF THE REASONS THIS is true is that we all live inside a great story, a never-ending story, the Greatest Story of all.

The Author of this great and true story is the Triune God. He has recorded for us this story in His inerrant and infallible Word, the Bible. *The Bible's narration of this story comprises the subject of this book.*

It is only when we see our life as part of this great story that everything starts to make sense. This is true because this great story aims to enable us to know its Author, who alone gives meaning to life. The more we comprehend the big picture of this great story, the more we can see ourselves inside it, and the more we will be living according to reality.

This great story is divided into four chapters:

	Chapter title	**Corresponding Bible section**
(I)	Creation	Genesis 1 – 2
(II)	Fall / Rebellion	Genesis 3
(III)	Redemption	Genesis 3:15 - Revelation 20
(IV)	Final Restoration	Revelation 21 – 22

In the center of this story, we find a Divine Person, the Lord Jesus Christ. He is the only and perfect revelation of God the Father to humanity (John 1:14, 18; 14:6, 9). Indeed, *the entire Bible's subject is Jesus.* It is not a coincidence that, in Hebrew, the name "Jesus" (i.e., Jehoshua) means *the Lord (YHWH) saves*[1] (cf. Matthew 1:21). It is no wonder, then, that if we were asked to give a one-word summary of the Bible's message, the glorious name of "Jesus" would suffice.

To substantiate the truth that the Lord Jesus is the absolute Hero of the greatest story of them all, the story that contains all other stories, it is worth answering the following *introductory questions:*

- **What does the Old Testament (OT from now on) mention about Jesus?**
- **What was Jesus doing during OT history?**

When we find the correct answers, we will be able to correctly discern the content of the four chapters that comprise the Greatest Story, the story the Bible tells.

What does the OT mention about Jesus?

Many people believe that the OT (the books of the Bible written *before* the Lord's incarnation, that is, written during the BC—Before Christ—era) has little, if anything, to say about Jesus. The testimonies of Jesus and His apostles correct this severe misunderstanding. These testimonies, which we are about to see, are not merely human opinions that can safely be ignored. They are the God-breathed answer the Bible gives to our first question.[2]

Jesus' testimony about the OT Scripture's content and meaning

In the last chapter of the Gospel according to Luke, we meet the risen Jesus on the day of His resurrection. He is walking alongside two of His disciples on the road to Emmaus. They do not recognize Him; they remain sad. He asks them what the matter is. They reply that they had hoped that Jesus was the one to redeem His people, but He was condemned to death and was crucified. And besides all this, it is now the third day since these things happened.

Jesus' response is unexpected. He calls them foolish, for they do not believe all that the prophets had written. So, they should have known from the OT scriptures that the Christ should suffer these things and enter into His glory (Luke 24:13-26).

For hours as they continue on their journey, Jesus interprets to them in *all* the OT Scriptures the things concerning Himself. When they arrived at the village and invited Him to eat with them, Luke records that their eyes were opened, they recognized Jesus, and He departed from among them.

Jesus chose to prevent His disciples from recognizing Him with their natural eyes during their travel together so that they would recognize the crucified and risen Lord and Savior through the Scriptures under His teaching. This is exactly what Jesus continues doing even to this day—He reveals Himself to His disciples through *all* the Scriptures. These two disciples' hearts were burning while Jesus was opening to them the Scriptures (Luke 24:32). When we also see, by faith, the Lord in the Scriptures, especially in the OT Scriptures, we too can experience this blessed spiritual heartburn.

As Luke continues his narration, we see Jesus suddenly appear among His gathered disciples and, once again, explain to them that *all* the Scriptures (i.e., the Law of Moses and the Prophets and the Psalms) speak about Him and that, indeed, *the Bible's central message is this: "that the Christ should suffer and on the third day rise from the dead, and that repentance for the forgiveness of sins should be proclaimed in his name to all nations ..."* (Luke 24:46-47).

It should be clear by now the Lord revealed to His disciples that *the entire Scripture's subject is the "Gospel",*[3] *the Good News,* namely the wonderful news concerning the person and work of the Lord Jesus Christ.

The apostles' testimony about the OT Scripture's content and meaning

By examining the writings of Jesus' disciples, we ascertain that they clearly perceived their Master's teaching and reverently followed His example, as evidenced by the fact that they, too, gave the same significance and meaning to the Scriptures. This evidence we will now present.

Testimony of the apostle Peter

In the book of the Acts of the Apostles, we see how the apostle Peter on the day of Pentecost (Acts 2) used the OT to explain the meaning of that day's events. He specifically proved that the Scriptures had foretold the resurrection of Jesus by quoting Psalm 16.

Indeed, throughout the book of Acts, we see Peter declaring *all the OT prophets gave testimony* that it is through faith in Jesus that forgiveness of sins is given (e.g., Acts 10:43).

Moreover, in his first epistle, Peter declared that the indwelling spirit of Christ had revealed to the OT prophets all the things concerning the sufferings of Christ and the glory that was to come (1 Pet. 1:10-12).

Testimony of the apostle Paul

Throughout the book of Acts, we see the apostle Paul reasoning with the Jews in the synagogues and proving from the OT scriptures that Jesus is the Christ, the long-awaited Messiah. (The title "Christ" is not Jesus' surname! The Greek word "Christos" is the translation into Greek of the Hebrew word "Mashiach", which means anointed.) Indeed, he proclaimed that Jesus was the prophesied Christ who had to suffer and rise from the dead (Acts 17:1-3).

Repeatedly, Paul claimed that his message is the same as the message of the OT prophets. In fact, at one point, he declared that *the summary of the message of Moses, the prophets, and the Psalms was that Christ had to suffer and then be raised from the dead* (Acts 26:22-23).

Testimony of the apostle John

The apostle John also realized the *absolute Christ-centeredness of the OT.* This is why he recorded the following words that Jesus addressed to the Jews: *"You search the Scriptures because you think that in them you have eternal life; and **it is they that bear witness about me,** yet you refuse to come to me that you may have life … For, if you believed Moses, you would believe me; for **he wrote of me**"* (John 5:39-40, 46, emphasis mine). What a marvelous truth! All the Scriptures bear witness to Jesus that we may come to Him and have life.

We have concisely shown that the apostles understood that all the Scriptures reveal Christ, and thus they confidently proclaimed Him from them. Their testimony and practice, then, unanimously accord with Jesus' teaching. Let us now turn to the second introductory question.

What was Jesus doing during OT history?

As the incarnate Lord said, Moses wrote about Him. Moses wrote *prophecies* about the coming savior, and he recorded *types,* namely symbols, which reveal Jesus and His work. Such symbols are, for example, the Tabernacle of the Testimony, the temple, the prophets, kings, priests, and the priests' sacrifices. But the most significant and frequent way with which Moses and all other OT authors constantly wrote about the Lord Jesus is *the recording of His real presence.* Indeed, Jesus is actively *present* on every page. He is the sent LORD (YHWH), the second person of the Trinity, the one who was always revealing the Father: *"No one has ever seen God; the only God, who is at the Father's side, **he has made him known**"* (John 1:18, emphasis mine).

According to John 1:18, no one has ever seen God the Father. At the same time, it is true that *during OT history* (the millennia preceding the birth of Jesus) we find recorded many meetings of God with people; we discover many instances where a Divine person communicated face to face with human beings. This dilemma is solved once one discerns that *it was the pre-incarnate Jesus, the eternal Word, who was revealing God the Father to people throughout the OT.* No one has ever seen God the Father face-to-face. Many people, however, saw the Lord Jesus many times and in many ways. This makes perfect sense once one realizes that the Lord Jesus was, is, and will always be the only way to God the Father (John 14:6). Jesus revealed the true God to people through dreams, the prophets, His presence inside the pillar of cloud, and His communication in human form with specific individuals (Christophanies—visible appearances of the pre-incarnate Christ).

This is why, in the eighth chapter of the Gospel according to John, we see Jesus saying to the Jews that Abraham saw Him face-to-face (John 8:56). The Lord Jesus says that Abraham saw His day and was glad because, beyond all the prophecies that Abraham already knew, it was the Lord who spoke to Abraham face-to-face (Gen. 15, 18). The reaction of His interlocutors proves that this is how they understood His words (cf. John 8:56-59). Jesus declared, *"I am,"* the Jews recognized that Jesus meant that He is the great I AM, the person who spoke with Moses out of the midst of the burning bush (Exod. 3:14), and, considering Him to be a blasphemer, they tried to kill Him.

The New Testament (NT from now on) authors took for granted that *the OT's theology is Trinitarian;* this is why the evangelist John stated, without further explanation, that Isaiah saw Jesus' glory (cf. John 12:38-41, which references the sixth chapter of Isaiah, where the prophet Isaiah recorded his resplendent vision of the Lord). Truly, *the Lord Jesus is the God of Israel.*

The real presence of the Son in the OT

So this is what Jesus was doing during OT history: He was present on every OT Scripture page, revealing the true God and fulfilling His plans.

Many people mistakenly think that Jesus resembles a substitute player anxiously waiting on the bench for the second half (the NT era) to participate in the match. Their primary understanding of Christ in the OT is one of prophecy, not presence. We have shown otherwise.

A.T. Hanson emphasized the importance of avoiding such mistaken approaches to the Bible when he wrote that the real presence of the pre-existent Christ in OT history is "the most important clue to the understanding of the NT exegesis of the OT."[4] Indeed, any effort to understand the Scriptures without building upon the interpretive foundation that our Lord and His apostles gave us will necessarily miss the mark. For, undeniably, the Lord Jesus Christ *is not* the Kappa and the Omega. He is *"the Alpha and the Omega, the first and the last, the beginning and the end"* (Rev. 22:13).

* * *

The Bible tells **one great story**

The Old Testament presents the Hero of the story, Yahweh, and promises that *He is the one who will save His people from their sins.* The New Testament reveals how Yahweh became incarnate and how He fulfilled all these astonishing promises. Not two separate stories, but one. The LORD (Yahweh) Jesus is the Hero of the entire Bible.

Jesus and His disciples gave us Christ-centered hermeneutical lenses, namely that the entire Bible reveals the living Christ. Keeping this in mind, we will now turn to the beginning of the Bible to study the contents of the first chapter of the greatest story, the chapter of Creation.

In the beginning, God created
the heavens and the earth.
The earth was without form and void,
and darkness was over the face of the
deep. And the Spirit of God was hovering
over the face of the waters.

Genesis 1:1-2

... the LORD God formed the man
of dust from the ground and
breathed into his nostrils the
breath of life, and the man
became a living creature.

Genesis 2:7

You rule the raging of the sea;
when its waves rise, you still them. ...
The heavens are yours;
the earth also is yours;
the world and all that is in it,
you have founded them.

Psalms 89:9, 11

The heavens declare
the glory of God,
and the sky above
proclaims his handiwork.

Psalm 19:1

1. CREATION

THE BIBLE BEGINS WITH THE CREATION OF THE WORLD. THE first chapters of Genesis contain the historical narration of how God created everything out of nothing by His powerful Word. We will examine what the Bible says about the identity of our Creator, and then we will study what creation reveals about its Creator and His plans.

The identity of our Creator

We have already seen that the Lord Jesus is actively present on every page of the Bible. We shouldn't be surprised, then, to learn that *Jesus is our Creator.* The NT tells us repeatedly and at key points that *God the Father created everything through God the Son, the Lord Jesus Christ.* Especially in his letter to the Colossians, the apostle Paul, exalting Jesus and exulting in His preeminence over all things, writes, *"[Jesus] is the image of the invisible God, the firstborn of all creation. For by him all things were created, in heaven and on earth, visible and invisible, whether thrones or dominions or rulers or authorities—**all things were created through him and for him.** And he is before all things, and in him all things hold together"* (Col. 1:15-17, emphasis mine).

In these verses, Paul explicitly states that all things were created through Christ, for Him, and that in Him all things hold together (cf. John 1:1-3, 14-17; Heb. 1:1-3). The Lord Jesus, then, is the Creator and Sustainer of the universe. "Blind luck," therefore, is a nonentity since the Lord governs all things. The cosmos is Christ's cosmos.

Our first ancestors rebelled against the Lord Jesus (Gen. 3), so it is fitting He should become our Redeemer also. This cosmic Christ is the only Savior. As Paul wrote, He is the beginning of the new humanity, of the new creation (Col. 1:18). Indeed, *creation and redemption are intimately tied together.* So close are they that salvation is described many times with the vocabulary of creation, e.g., *"... if anyone is in Christ, he is a new creation"* (2 Cor. 5:17; cf. with 2 Cor. 4:6). Indeed, in its essence, salvation is nothing less than union and communion through faith with the risen Christ, the firstborn from the dead, *the beginning of the new creation.*

This connection between creation and redemption goes further back in time than we would have expected. The three Divine persons had decided the plan of redemption even before the foundation of the world (Rev. 13:8; 1 Pet. 1:18-20; 2 Tim. 1:8-10; Eph. 1:3-7).

This realization leads to the following observation—when the Lord Jesus created the world, He created the stage of the drama of redemption. Namely, the stage in which He Himself would come to redeem His people from their sins in the fullness of time.

The Bible's many allusions to nature are not merely an afterthought of the divine Author. The incarnate Lord did not simply look around seeking aids to illustrate His teaching. The Lord Jesus designed His creation with the purpose of using its details as a supervisory aid to teach sinners the truth about the way of salvation and the great Savior.

Creation: A supervisory aid to understanding redemption

Let us examine just a few aspects of our world in the light of Scripture to find out what creation is meant to teach us about our Creator and His plan of redemption:

Objects like a hammer, milk, bread, gold, and honey describe angles of the power, usefulness, preciousness, and sweetness of God's word.

Sheep remind us that we are lost without Jesus, the Good Shepherd of the sheep.

The birds of the sky and the lilies of the field reveal the wonderful care and providence of our heavenly Father.

Bread points to the Lord as the one who gives true life and sustains it.

Light gives us a faint picture of the greatness of the Majesty of the Lord's Glory. Also, light displays the power of Jesus to drive away the darkness.

Water is a symbol of the Holy Spirit who, like water, cleanses, refreshes, renews, and quenches humanity's thirst for life.

And it is worth wondering, how did the Lord Jesus feel knowing He was signing His death sentence while creating the trees and metals His rebellious creatures would use to crucify Him?

Examining the alternations of the seasons, we see that:

- Summer corresponds to creation
- Autumn corresponds to the fall of humankind
- Winter is reminiscent of darkness, alienation, and death, i.e., the effects of the fall
- Spring is the celebration of the resurrection
- And after all this, summer comes to remind us of the final restoration, of the coming new heaven and earth, which Christians long for.

The sun's apparent motion in the sky and the alternation of night and day is a dynamic image that daily proclaims the glory of Jesus' death and resurrection.

Our need for sleep is also an image of our own death and resurrection in Christ.

When seen through the lens of the Bible, the plant's seeds become an image of the death that must precede the resurrection (John 12:24).

People's relationships with each other (marriage, parent-child relationships, and brotherly bonds) reveal facets of the relationship we can have with the Triune God.

The almost miraculous transformation of the caterpillar into a butterfly serves as a small picture of the incredible miracle that happens when, at the moment of new birth, the spiritually dead person is given true, eternal life.

Creation reveals the greatness of its Creator

And of course, just as a painter's work reveals things about himself, so creation reveals the perfect attributes of its Creator:

- Almighty (He created and now sustains everything by His powerful word)
- All wise (only an infinitely intelligent mind could design the perfect harmony and complexity that marks our world at every level)
- Incredibly creative (the amazing variety of flora and fauna speaks for itself)
- Exceedingly generous (thousands upon thousands of stars adorn the night sky)
- Absolutely beautiful (creation's beauty is but a faint reflection of the Creator's beauty)
- Supremely good (He created this world even though He knew that He would have to become incarnate to die upon a Roman cross).

The Creator Lord Jesus and science

Nowadays, some people mistakenly believe that the scientific endeavor is incompatible with the Christian faith. Nothing could be further from the truth. On the contrary, the revelation that the Lord Jesus created the universe and maintains it is the basis for the existence of science. This is true because, *for the edifice of science to stand, specific foundations are needed, including particular assumptions.* Namely, that laws govern nature, that these laws apply throughout the universe, and that the laws of nature remain constant over time. Therefore, one must believe that the laws of nature will continue to apply in the future in the same way they did in the past.

Without these assumptions, the enterprise of science would be completely impossible. Let us think about why it is so. If the laws of nature were to change tomorrow, the results of all past experiments would instantly lose all value, as the various scientific laws derived from past data would crumble and could no longer predict anything about the future. The existence of science, then, depends entirely on assumptions that the scientific method itself (empirical verification of a hypothesis through repeated experimental observations) has absolutely no way of proving.

The truth is that a God-denying scientist is forced to accept science's most fundamental assumptions in blind faith. In stark contrast, a Christian scientist has every reason to hope that his research will be crowned with success because he knows that the living God created the universe. Therefore, he expects to find order and harmony in the universe and life-preserving laws in operation. He also knows that the Lord sustains His creation with reason and steadfastness. God does not change, and thus, He rules the universe consistently throughout the centuries and millennia (Gen. 8:22; Jer. 33:25).

This was the worldview of scientists such as Johannes Kepler and Louis Pasteur. Kepler (1571 – 1630) was a mathematician and astronomer. He was one of the most prominent representatives of the scientific revolution of the seventeenth century. He is considered the founder of celestial mechanics and modern optics. He wrote:

"Since we astronomers are priests of the highest God in regard to the book of nature, it befits us to be thoughtful, not of the glory of our minds, but rather, above all else, of the glory of God"[5]

"Those laws [of nature] are within the grasp of the human mind; God wanted us to recognize them by creating us after His own image so that we could share in His own thoughts."[6]

Pasteur (1822 – 1895) is the founder of microbiology and immunology. He wrote:

"The more I study nature, the more I stand amazed at the work of the Creator. Science brings men nearer to God."

"Little science takes you away from God but more of it takes you to Him."[7]

These quotations are just the tip of the iceberg, as similar statements mark the works of most founders of modern science.[8] It is evident, then, how unhistorical and unsubstantiated the claims of those who try to attack Christianity are by saying that it supposedly conflicts with (operational, experimental) science.

In fact, *any view of science that does not begin with the Lord Jesus is fundamentally flawed since everything exists from Him and for Him.* Everything is worth doing, as Kepler said, for the glory of God (1 Cor. 10:31; Col. 3:17). The purpose of the world's exploration, then, should be the discovery and admiration of its Creator's glory. This doesn't mean that an atheist cannot be a good scientist as far as results are concerned. However, it means that the only reason he can be successful is that he operates on borrowed capital, with assumptions that his materialistic worldview cannot support. And most importantly, it means that this person's greatest need is the redemption of Christ so that he can finally begin to live in spiritual reality. And not just this person, but everyone who uses God's gifts without thanking Him has the same desperate need, Jesus' redemption (Rom. 1:18-23).

The purpose of humankind's creation reveals the purpose of Redemption

The description of redemption as a new creation leads to one more observation: The purpose of humankind's creation can shed light on the purpose of redemption. Let us, then, examine what the purpose of humankind's creation reveals about the purpose of redemption.

The Triune God created humanity (male and female) in His image and likeness (Gen. 1:26-27). The Lord miraculously created Adam from the dust of the ground and then Eve from Adam's rib, as narrated in Genesis' second chapter. The image of God the Father has always been the Lord Jesus (see Col. 1:15; 2 Cor. 4:4). *The purpose of human-ity's creation, then, was to fill the earth with images (mirrors) that would reflect the glory of God.* This plan would take place as the first humans, who were created in the image of Christ, would obey God's command and multiply (Gen. 1:26-28).

Humankind was created in the image of Christ, by Christ. He is the Lord God whose footsteps Adam and Eve heard in paradise (Gen. 3:8). We have been created, all humankind in Adam, to be like the Lord Jesus, i.e., to know and enjoy the company of God the Father, as He Himself has done from all eternity, and to reflect God's beauty and holiness, as the Lord does.

But when the first people believed the devil's lie, the mirror was shuttered. People became self-centered and unbelieving; they now chose to listen to the devil rather than to God.

The pre-eminent image of God, Jesus Christ, became incarnate to show us what it means to be God's true image and to transform us once again into what we were made to be, mirrors that reflect His beauty.

Here, then, is the purpose of redemption, of the new creation—the Lord Jesus came to do everything necessary to re-create His people to be like His own image (see Col. 3:10; Rom. 8:29). This process starts in a person's life at the moment of regeneration. From then on, Christians are grad-ually transformed into the glorious image of Jesus as they see Him with the eyes of faith: *"And we all, with unveiled face, beholding the glory of the Lord, **are being transformed into the same image** from one degree of glory to another"* (2 Cor. 3:18, emphasis mine).

Christians behold Jesus as they read the Scriptures with the antici-pation to meet Him there since the Bible's pages shine forth the light of the gospel of the glory of Christ (see 2 Cor. 4:4-6). We were made to be mirrors, so we become like what we love, we become like what we worship.

All Christians' transformation will be perfected in the new heavens and the new earth, which Jesus will bring in His second coming. Then our redemption will be complete (Rom. 8:23), and *"... the earth will be filled with the knowledge of the glory of the LORD ... "* (Hab. 2:14).

* * *

We live in a world where we are both spectators and participants. The perfect Hero is the crucified and risen Savior, the Lord Jesus. He has created everyone; thus, everyone is called to live with Him and for Him.

Creation's expected outcome, therefore, would be the creature's close communion with its Creator. This was the case in the Garden of Eden, where everything was very good (Gen. 1:31). However, the prospect of such a close and loving relationship with the Lord seems unreasonable today. In fact, the mere mention of such a possibility causes the ridicule of many.

We have already mentioned the cause of humankind's tragic separation from the Lord—our first ancestors' rebellion, also known as original sin or man's fall. This disastrous fall is the cause of all decay, alienation, misery, wickedness, disease, and physical and spiritual death that surrounds us. The fall explains the existence of evil in our world; it is the root of all the evilness that plagues every human heart and marks every society.

The greatest story's next chapter presents humankind's colossal Fall from Grace and its horrific effects. Perhaps many would be tempted to skip this chapter. Nevertheless, a proper appreciation of the fall is necessary to understand how monstrous sin is. The knowledge of sin's heinousness enables us to realize why nothing less than the blood of God's own Son could redeem us.

And the LORD God commanded the man, saying,
"You may surely eat of every tree of the garden,
but of the tree of the knowledge of good and evil
you shall not eat, for in the day that you eat of it
you shall surely die."

Genesis 2:16-17

[The LORD] drove out the man, and at the east
of the Garden of Eden he placed the cherubim
and a flaming sword that turned every way to
guard the way to the tree of life.

Genesis 3:24

Yea cannot slander human nature;
it is worse than words can paint it.

C. H. Spurgeon—"Salt-Cellars"

It is only against the pitch blackness of the night that
we see the glory of the stars. And it is only against the
pitch blackness of man's radical depravity that we can
begin to see the glories of the Gospel.

Paul Washer

Psychology keeps trying to vindicate human nature.
History keeps undermining the effort.

Mason Cooley

2. FALL

IN THE BEGINNING OF CREATION, IN THE GARDEN OF EDEN, all was very well; the first humans enjoyed each other's company and, in unison, enjoyed the company of their Creator, the Lord Jesus. They saw Him face-to-face, and they walked with Him. There wasn't any pain, sorrow, loneliness, sickness, or death *because there was no sin. That is, there was no disobedience to the commands of the Lord.* And yet, even though those first people had everything, they believed the devil's lie, who, in essence, told them that the Lord Jesus was not enough. And so, the first people turned their backs on their Creator; they disobeyed His commands while knowing the consequences; *they committed treason of cosmic proportions* by abandoning the One who is both the true life and the source of life. The result was spiritual and physical death. It could not be otherwise since they chose to cut themselves off from the Lord Jesus, from life itself. Outside of Jesus, there is nothing but darkness, destruction, and eternal death.

This terrible disobedience, this *horrific fall*, affects every human being. It impacts all of humanity, as every descendant of Adam is born with Adam's fallen, sinful nature. As we are all born united with Adam, we are born as a dry branch in Adam's fallen, dead tree (Rom. 5:12-21; 1 Cor. 15:20-23). As Genesis states, *"This is the book of the generations of Adam. When God created man, he made him in the likeness of God. Male and female he created them, and he blessed them and named them Man when they were created. When Adam had lived 130 years,* **he fathered a son in his own likeness, after his image,** *and named him Seth"* (Gen. 5:1-3, emphasis mine).

Seth, the son of Adam, was born in the image of fallen Adam, in his likeness. From the first moment of his existence, *Seth was a shattered mirror.* This brokenness is equally true of all of Adam's descendants to this day.

This news is not at all flattering. What is important, however, *is not* what sounds pleasing to our ears and what does not, *but what is true.* We desperately need the truth to start living according to reality. And the truth about us is far worse than we would dare to admit even to our own selves. The picture that God's word paints about the condition of fallen man is thoroughly pitch-black. No other philosophy, ideology, or way of thinking has ever presented a darker view of fallen humankind than the Bible gives.

The necessity of understanding the magnitude and effects of the fall of humanity

We need to understand the magnitude of the fall and its present consequences for the following reasons:

1. Because only then will sinful man be able to see his absolute need for salvation. Only when we realize our misery are our attempts at self-justification destroyed.
2. Only after seeing the truth about oneself is one willing to turn to Christ.
3. Only when one realizes from what condemnation and at what cost Jesus saved him one ceases to trust anywhere else and trusts in Christ alone.
4. Because this truth leads to gratitude, love, praise, devotion, and obedience to the wonderful Lord Jesus.

Extent and magnitude of the Fall of man[9]

The Bible leaves no doubt about how destructive this first act of humanity's disobedience was. Adam was God's vice-regent over material creation (Gen. 1:26-28). That is why his fall, his rebellion, resulted in the entire creation's fall with him. Due to man's sin, corruption, disease, pain, and death entered creation. That is why now nature groans, waiting for the time of its deliverance from the bondage of decay. This deliverance will occur when the Lord Jesus, in His second coming, will establish the new heavens and the new earth. Those who love Him await this final restoration eagerly (Rom. 8:18-25).

In addition to the repercussions of human disobedience on material creation, it has already been stated that the fall's *moral consequences* extend to every descendant of Adam and Eve. No one in the history of humanity, except the Lord Jesus, the God-man, has ever lived obediently to God. This moral inability directly results from the protoplasts' fall—their choice corrupted their nature and polluted every aspect of their existence with sin. Consequently, all their descendants (i.e., all humankind) inherited this fallen, sinful nature. This assertion I will now substantiate, and then proceed to succinctly outline God's solution to humankind's sin and misery.

What is the truth about man's fallen, sinful nature?

Let us see God's verdict just before the flood of Noah, a judgment that succinctly reveals the truth about sinful humanity's character: *"The LORD saw that the wickedness of man was great in the earth, and that every intention of the thoughts of his heart was only evil continually"* (Gen. 6:5).

All the thoughts of the human heart are always and only evil. This sinful condition is what God sees when He looks into people's hearts. We may think that there are good people. Indeed, on the horizontal, human level, when we compare ourselves with others, we do see people performing good deeds, and helping their fellow human beings. However, things are quite different on the vertical, divine level since God sees the heart. He sees sinful motives. He sees that even the best deed is done by people who are cut off from Jesus Christ and hate the true God, even if they are unwilling to admit it (Rom. 1:30; John 3:18-20, 15:18-25).

When does humanity's sinful nature begin its operation?

Humanity's wickedness grieves God's heart. So much so that He decided to blot out the entire human race (except Noah and his family) by the catastrophic global flood, which has come to be known as Noah's flood (Gen. chs. 6 to 8). After the flood's description, Genesis records the following thoughts of God: *"... the LORD said in his heart, 'I will never again curse the ground because of man, for the intention of man's heart is evil from his youth. Neither will I ever again strike down every living creature as I have done'"* (Gen. 8:21).

God stated that He would never again destroy the earth by the waters of the flood (8:21, 9:11), even though *"the intention of man's heart is evil from his youth."* These words teach us that the wickedness of man remains even after the flood. In fact, God tells us that the intentions of man's heart are evil *"from his youth."* We are born sinful, and our wickedness begins operating from our earliest stages of existence.

Does our inherited sinfulness exempt us from being accountable for our sins?

David knew that he was conceived and born in sin: *"Behold, I was brought forth in iniquity, and in sin did my mother conceive me"* (Ps. 51:5). This knowledge, however, did not lead him to try to justify himself for his sins; on the contrary, it led him to keenly feel his guilt before a holy God and his need for forgiveness. We see David's confession in Psalm 51, which he wrote after repenting of his adultery with Bathsheba. In harmony with the rest of the Bible, this psalm teaches that *man, in his inherited fallen state and corruption, is always accountable to God both for what he is and for his every choice.*

Is anyone born "good"?

No one is born "good," deep down. The admittedly unsettling truth for every human being is this—we are born guilty before God and deeply corrupt, with a fallen sinful nature, which continually leads to evil. There is no exception (other than the Lord Jesus) to humanity's sinfulness, as we learn both from the OT and NT Scriptures:

> *"Enter not into judgment with your servant, for **no one living is righteous before you.**"* (Ps. 143:2, emphasis mine)

> *"And [Jesus] said, 'What comes out of a person is what defiles him. For **from within, out of the heart of man, come** evil thoughts, sexual immorality, theft, murder, adultery, coveting, wickedness, deceit, sensuality, envy, slander, pride, foolishness. **All these evil things come from within, and they defile a person.**'"* (Mark 7:20-23, emphasis mine)

> *"For we have already charged that all, both Jews and Greeks, are under sin, as it is written: **'None is righteous, no, not one;** no one understands; no one seeks for God. All have turned aside; together **they have become worthless; no one does good, not even one'** ... for **all have sinned** and fall short of the glory of God ..."* (Rom. 3:9b-12, 23, emphasis mine)

The Holy Spirit guided the apostle Paul to state that there is **not one** who does good, there is **not one** who seeks the true God, there is **not one** who understands. Paul comes to this conclusion after the first two chapters of his letter to the Romans, in which he carefully builds his argument to conclude that *"no one is righteous"* (Rom. 3:10b, emphasis mine). In two words: *Radical depravity.*

Suppose someone believes that the above description doesn't accurately portray them. In that case, I think the following question should suffice: Dear reader, imagine it were possible to record on a video all your thoughts, desires, feelings, and motives that went through your heart the past week, along with all your words and deeds; if somebody told you that this video would be projected in front of your friends and acquaintances, how would you react then?

How extensive is humankind's depravity?

Experientially we are not as bad as we could be. Praise God because have not committed even more sins, even more crimes against God and people. And yet, sin has poisoned every aspect of our existence, nothing has been left unaffected, so *our depravity is total.* Human existence resembles a glass of pure water. If we put a spoonful of strong poison in it and mix it, who would want to take even a sip? Such pollution is true of us, too. Sin has infected every part of our being: (1) our mind and heart are deceitful, (2) our desires are corrupted, and (3) our will is enslaved.

Total depravity of mind, desires, will

1. Depravity of people's heart/mind (deceitful):

The Genesis verses (6:5, 8:21) and Jesus' words (Mark 7:20-23), which have already been quoted, depict the corruption of the unregenerate man's thoughts and heart. We can also add the words of the prophet Jeremiah and the apostle Paul, respectively:

> *"The heart is deceitful above all things, and desperately sick; who can understand it?"* (Jer. 17:9)

> *"Now this I say and testify in the Lord, that you must no longer walk as the Gentiles do,* **in the futility of their minds.** *They are darkened in their understanding, alienated from the life of God because of the ignorance that is in them, due to their* **hardness of heart.***"* (Eph. 4:17-18, emphasis mine)

These verses teach that people's difficulty is not intellectual; that, supposedly, there is no evidence for belief in God. The Bible says that all are without excuse since they are confronted daily by creation, in which the attributes of its Creator are indelibly engraved (Rom. 1:19-20).

People's difficulty is entirely moral, as they choose to live in ignorance because of their hardness of heart. A heart that, until Christ with His Spirit changes it, is *"deceitful above all things"* (Jer. 17:9).

2. Depravity of people's desires (corrupted):

Since the human heart is deceitful and corrupted, it is like a factory that constantly produces idols and evil desires. Thus, the desires of sinful man are also corrupt. *We are not sinners because we sin; we sin because we are sinners,* and sin springs from within us, just as the apostle Paul and the Lord Jesus, respectively, teach:

> *"And **you were dead** in the trespasses and sins in which you once walked, following the course of this world, following the prince of the power of the air, the spirit that is now at work in the sons of disobedience—among whom we all once lived **in the passions of our flesh, carrying out the desires of the body and the mind,** and **were by nature children of wrath,** like the rest of mankind."* (Eph. 2:1-3, Apostle Paul, emphasis mine)

> *"You are of your father the devil, and **your will is to do your father's desires.** He was a murderer from the beginning, and does not stand in the truth, because there is no truth in him. When he lies, he speaks out of his own character, for he is a liar and the father of lies."* (John 8:44, Jesus Christ, emphasis mine)

Devilish desires spring from humanity's fallen nature and lead to trespasses and sins.

3. Depravity of people's will (enslaved):

The will of man is a "servant" of his desires. What man desires most at any given time, this he will always choose. And because man's desires are corrupt, *his will is enslaved to sin,* leading him to choose evil. This is the truth that the Lord reveals in Scripture about fallen, sinful man:

*"So Jesus said to the Jews who had believed him, 'If you abide in my word, you are truly my disciples, and you will know the truth, and the truth will set you free.' They answered him, 'We are offspring of Abraham and have never been enslaved to anyone. How is it that you say, 'You will become free'?' Jesus answered them, 'Truly, truly, I say to you, **everyone who practices sin is a slave to sin.** The slave does not remain in the house forever; the son remains forever. So if the Son sets you free, you will be free indeed'"* (John 8:31-36, emphasis mine).

People's wills are in bondage to sin and, thus, not free. People slavishly follow their fallen, sinful desires by doing what they want. The problem is that what they wish to do is sinful until God regenerates man and gives him a new heart. What is even worse is that they baptize their slavery as freedom. They say, "Follow your heart, do what you want." They think they are free. However, true freedom is to desire what is good and be able to do it. As Jesus says: *"If the Son sets you free, you will be free indeed"* (John 8:36).

Those that claim the opposite, namely that the will of fallen, natural man (that is, one who does not have the Spirit of God, who has not been born again) is supposedly free, go against the words of Christ by preferring human traditions[10] (cf. John 3:19; 2 Tim. 2:25-26; 2 Pet. 2:19; Titus 3:3).

This is the wretched condition of all of Adam's descendants—born guilty, by nature children of wrath (Eph. 2:3), and very corrupt. We are created in the image of God, but the mirror has been shattered into a thousand pieces. Broken mirrors, glorious ruins; indeed, as the apostle Paul says: *"For I know that nothing good dwells in me, that is, in my flesh"* (Rom. 7:18a). *Being omniscient, God sees that there is no trace of genuine goodness in fallen, unregenerate humanity; man's heart is deceitful, his desires are corrupt, and his will is enslaved.*

Can fallen man do anything to change himself?

The natural man's wretched condition is utterly hopeless because he cannot improve it in any way. As the prophet Jeremiah wrote so graphically: *"Can the Ethiopian change his skin or the leopard his spots? Then also you can do good who are accustomed to do evil"* (Jer. 13:23).

The enslaved sinful man cannot change his condition; he cannot free himself from the bondage of sin; he cannot transform his nature. That which is born of the flesh is flesh (John 3:6). In the NT, the term "flesh" usually refers to man's fallen, sinful nature. Man does not come into the world being merely seriously ill. *Man comes into the world being spiritually dead;* as the apostle Paul wrote: *"And you, who **were dead** in your trespasses and the uncircumcision of your flesh, **God made alive together with him,** having forgiven us all our trespasses ... "* (Col. 2:13, emphasis mine; cf. Eph. 2:1-5).

Can the fallen, natural man please God?

The Bible is clear that the necessary prerequisite for anyone to please God is to have true faith: *"And **without faith it is impossible to please [God],** for whoever would draw near to God must believe that he exists and that he rewards those who seek him"* (Heb. 11:6, emphasis mine). Anyone who does not trust in the Savior Christ and in Him alone can never please the true God, no matter what he thinks is true of himself.

Do people seek the living God on their own?

According to the Bible, no one seeks after God. Since the day Adam and Eve tried to hide from the Lord in the garden (Gen.3:8), people have run to hide away from the true God (Rom. 3:10-12). People don't want to face the true God, just as a thief doesn't want to meet a police officer. People may be deeply "spiritual" and follow various religions and false "gods." Still, all this is nothing more than fig leaves, which they use as a cover to try to quiet their consciences and continue to stay away from the Triune God. Only the miracle of regeneration by the Holy Spirit causes man's disposition and attitude to change.

The natural man's disposition toward God

Then, what is the natural (non-born again) man's disposition toward God? People are enemies of God (Col. 1:21; Rom. 5:8-10) and alienated from Him (Eph. 2:11-13). They are under the righteous wrath of God, as they are by nature children of wrath (Eph. 2:3, John 3:36). In fact, the whole of man's existence is enmity toward God since he does not want and cannot submit to His law. We would do well to heed the words of the apostle Paul:

> *"For to set the mind on the flesh is death, but to set the mind on the Spirit is life and peace. For **the mind that is set on the flesh is hostile to God, for it does not submit to God's law; indeed, it cannot.** Those who are in the flesh cannot please God. You, however, are not in the flesh but in the Spirit, if in fact the Spirit of God dwells in you. Anyone who does not have the Spirit of Christ does not belong to him."* (Rom. 8:6-9, emphasis mine)

Fleshy, natural people do not have the Spirit of Christ; they do not belong to Christ, and neither do they want to belong to Him.

Can natural man understand and accept the gospel of Christ on his own?

Such is man's enmity toward God, and such is the dislike of the flesh toward the glory of God, that the natural man, while being able to comprehend the historical events of the Crucifixion and Resurrection of Jesus, cannot and does not want to see in himself anything of value. This blindness is owed to his darkened mind, which causes the gospel, namely the Cross of Christ, to seem foolish. The apostle Paul stated in 1 Corinthians 2:14 that *"The natural person does not accept the things of* *the Spirit of God, for **they are folly to him, and he is not able to understand them** because they are spiritually discerned"* (emphasis mine). When read in context, the things of the Spirit, which the natural person does not accept and cannot understand, are the *"word of the cross,"* the gospel (cf. 1 Cor. 1:18).

The natural man is alive to sin but dead to God. Therefore, the gospel appears to him to be foolishness. (*"… the word of the cross is **folly** to those who are perishing, but to us who are being saved it is the power of God"* – 1 Cor. 1:18, emphasis mine; cf. 2 Cor. 4:4-6; Matt. 16:15-17; John 6:63.)

The condition of fallen man is horrifically tragic and wretched. And how immense is his corrupt heart's ability to avoid the truth through self-deception!

The solution to humankind's sin and misery

The solution to our misery is entirely outside of us. We owe it all to God. If He had not done everything for us, if we'd had to add even one iota to Christ's work, we would have been eternally lost. It is *God the Father* who brings people to Christ (John 6:44, 63-65). It is *Christ* who, through the Cross and the Resurrection, secured for His people the forgiveness of their sins and the gift of the Holy Spirit. It is the *Holy Spirit* who opens blind eyes and gives life to the dead to come to Christ (2 Cor. 4:4-6; 1 Cor. 4:7, 12:3). God, through His Spirit, grants repentance (2 Tim. 2:25-26) and faith (Phil. 1:29) so that we may receive Christ. And then, united by faith with the source of life Himself, we begin to live truly.

We owe it all to the grace of the Triune God so that all glory may be given only to Him. (One of the rallying cries of the religious reformation was "Soli Deo Gloria"—Glory to God alone.) And when a Christian understands how amazing God's grace is, he is filled with gratitude, joy, and love for the true God, and he boasts not in the slightest in himself but in the Lord and His cross. The Bible emphatically teaches that salvation is not a result of human works (even if these are Spirit-wrought), and thus no one can boast before God. On the contrary, Christians are repeatedly instructed to boast in the Lord, as the following passages illustrate (cf. Rom. 3:23-27; Gal. 6:14-15).

> *"But God chose what is foolish in the world to shame the wise; God chose what is weak in the world to shame the strong; God chose what is low and despised in the world, even things that are not, to bring to nothing things that are, so that no human being might boast in the presence of God. And **because of him you are in Christ Jesus,** who became to us wisdom from God, righteousness and sanctification and redemption, so that, as it is written, **'Let the one who boasts, boast in the Lord.'"***
> (1 Cor. 1:27-31, emphasis mine)

> *"For by grace you have been saved through faith. And this is not your own doing; it is the gift of God, **not a result of works, so that no one may boast."*** (Eph. 2:8-9, emphasis mine)

Indeed, salvation is by God's grace *alone.* Since we are in such a desperate situation, no other way could ever be enough. We do not need someone who will try to help us save ourselves; we need someone who will save us from beginning to end. We must die with Christ on the cross so that, united with Him through faith, we may be resurrected with Him in newness of life. No improvement of our sinful nature could ever be enough; nothing less than regeneration (new birth) will suffice (John 3:1-8).

Dear reader, if you do not belong to Christ, you are spiritually dead, lost in darkness. Nothing good dwells in you. You cannot change yourself. Look to the great Savior and liberator, Christ, and plead with Him to save you from God's righteous wrath and sin's bondage. He is the Only One who is willing and able to save sinful people like us. *He, the Lord Jesus, is your only hope.*

The Heidelberg Catechism on man's misery

Undoubtedly, the biblical truth concerning the fall of man and its consequences is not pleasing to people's ears. This observation is even more applicable to modern people, who believe that they are essentially good and cherish autonomy and self-determination as their highest values. But even Christians find it difficult to accept the image that the Bible paints of the tragic condition of fallen man, particularly when they encounter this truth for the first time. However, historically, this teaching has always been the theology of the reformed church. To establish this claim, it is worth quoting the relevant questions and answers from the *Heidelberg Catechism's* first section, which is suitably titled "Of Man's Misery." This catechism, written around 1563 AD, stands out for its warm and worshipful character. Its value is highlighted by the fact that all the churches resulting from the sixteenth-century religious reformation accepted it as one of their doctrinal standards. Even to this day, it remains widely in use.

HEIDELBERG CATECHISM[11]

Section I – Of Man's Misery

Question 3. Whence knowest thou thy misery?
Answer: Out of the Law of God.

Question 4. What does the Law of God require of us?
Answer: Christ teaches us in sum, Matthew 22: "Thou shalt love the Lord thy God with all thy heart, and with all thy soul, and with all thy mind, and with all thy strength. This is the first and great commandment. And the second is like unto it, thou shalt love thy neighbor as thyself. On these two commandments hang all the law and the prophets."

Question 5. Canst thou keep all this perfectly?

Answer: No, for I am prone by nature to hate God and my neighbor.

Question 6. Did God create man thus wicked and perverse?

Answer: No, but God created man good and after His own image, that is, in righteousness and true holiness, that he might rightly know God his Creator, heartily love Him, and live with Him in eternal blessedness, to praise and glorify Him.

Question 7. Whence then comes this depraved nature of man?

Answer: From the fall and disobedience of our first parents, Adam and Eve, in Paradise, whereby our nature became so corrupt that we are all conceived and born in sin.

Question 8. But are we so depraved that we are wholly incapable of any good and prone to all evil?

Answer: Yes, unless we are born again by the Spirit of God.

How to relate to those who are lost in sin

As the Holy Spirit convicts us of sin and enlightens us to see the truth, we come to our senses concerning our condition before God. This experiential knowledge is meant to lead us to humility. And then we can relate to lost people with *compassion and kindness*. The apostle Paul, in Titus 3:1-3, commands believers to have such a disposition. Paul uses the past tense to say that Christians were once slaves to their evil desires, as those who do not yet know Christ still are. And his argument is this: *Because* you were also in this sinful state (v. 3), now be submissive to the authorities and show meekness to everyone (v. 1-2). In essence, he says: You were no better than others; Christ saved you; therefore, treat those still lost in sin with kindness.

The greatest act of *kindness* toward lost people *is* the proclamation of the gospel. The hearing of the Good News is the means God has appointed for the salvation of spiritually dead people (Rom. 10:13-17). In the following verses in his epistle to Titus, the apostle Paul presents the gospel and the blessings it bestows on those who receive it with faith:

> *"But when the goodness and loving kindness of God our Savior appeared,* **he saved us, not because of works done by us in righteousness, but according to his own mercy, by the washing of regeneration and renewal of the Holy Spirit, whom he poured out on us richly through Jesus Christ our Savior,** *so that being justified by his grace we might become heirs according to the hope of eternal life."* (Titus 3:4-7, emphasis mine)

If this passage seems somewhat condensed, it's because it is. Paul has already instructed in depth his disciple Titus in the past, and, in this paragraph, he only briefly reminds him of this glorious message. Indeed, in these verses, we find a good summary of the way and purpose of Redemption. *Redemption is the subject matter of the greatest story's next chapter.* Let us turn to it and unpack God's eternal plan. How astonishing, when all seemed lost because of the Fall, the Triune God had already planned the salvation of His people from their sins!

41

If the Lord's bearing our sin
for us is not the gospel,
I have no gospel to preach. ...
The heart of the gospel is redemption,
and the essence of redemption is the
substitutionary sacrifice of Christ.

C. H. Spurgeon

Jesus Christ did not come into this
world to make bad people good;
he came into this world
to make dead people live.

Lee Strobel

You contribute nothing to your salvation
except the sin that made it necessary.

Jonathan Edwards

The Gospel does not call us to receive Christ
as an addition to our life, but *as* our life.

Paul Washer

*Jesus said to her, "I am the resurrection and the life.
Whoever believes in me, though he die, yet shall he live ... "*

John 11:25

*I have been crucified with Christ. It is no
longer I who live, but Christ who lives in me.*

Galatians 2:20a

3. THE STORY OF REDEMPTION

THE OT IS DIVIDED INTO THE LAW OF MOSES (I.E., THE PEN-
tateuch, the first five books of the OT), the Prophets, and the Psalms,
as the Lord Jesus confirms (Luke 24:44). In this chapter, we will follow
this threefold structure. As we see the story of redemption unfold, we
will focus on how each of these three sections reveals the Savior. I encourage every reader to examine all the referenced Scripture passages
"to see if these things are so" (Acts 17:11).

The Savior in the Pentateuch

God designed the plan for the redemption of His people from the fall's
terrible results even before the creation of the world. He puts it into
effect immediately after their fall into sin.

The Lord Jesus runs to find His rebellious creatures (Gen. 3:8).
Adam and Eve feel their shame, so they try to hide from the Lord and
cover up their nakedness (which now reflects their guilt before God)
by sewing fig leaves. Their attempt to hide from the One who knows
everything is utterly vain.

The Lord had warned them of the consequences of sin—spiritual
and bodily death. He will enforce the punishment since He is always
faithful to His word. And yet, even before He announces the sentence
to Adam and Eve, He curses the serpent and, by these words, Christ
declares that one of Eve's descendants (her seed) would come and crush
the head of the serpent: *"I will put enmity between you and the woman,
and between your offspring and her offspring; **he shall bruise your head,
and you shall bruise his heel"*** (Gen. 3:15, emphasis mine).

This is the first promise given after Adam and Eve ate the forbidden
fruit. Theologians call it the *protoevangelium* (or first gospel) because

this verse contains the first promise of redemption. *Everything else in the Bible flows from the words of Genesis 3:15.*

Indeed, the protoevangelium reveals the way of redemption—a savior will come and conquer man's enemy at immense personal cost. From now on, the story focuses on the fulfillment of the *promise* contained in the Lord's words to the snake. *The entire OT narration's goal is to reveal how this Divine offspring/seed will come and crush the snake's head* (a mere mortal man could never defeat Satan, the ancient serpent—Rev. 12:9). All the OT stories are related to this promise. And under this light are we to read them, considering their broader context. These stories do not primarily intend to give us moral lessons. That is why they should *not* be read as if they are similar to Aesop's fables. Their purpose is to show us who the promised Savior is, His character, and how He will save His people from their sin.

When Genesis 3 is read in this light, we observe that Adam and Eve should be considered the first Christians. They spoke face-to-face with the Lord Jesus and trusted in His promise, which was enough (see Gen. 3:20 & 4:1 for the manifestations of their faith). *All human beings were saved, are saved, and will be saved, for as long as this world endures, through faith alone in the Lord Jesus Christ alone.* The first people knew their need for a sacrifice; they knew that blood had to be shed before a man could draw near God. Indeed, they instructed their children, Cain and Abel, to offer sacrifices. Yet only Abel's offer was accepted by God, for he alone provided it by faith (Heb. 11:4). The Lord Himself taught Adam and Eve about the need for sacrifices while giving them the first insight into how sinners were to be saved. We read that before they were expelled from paradise, *"... the LORD God made for Adam and for his wife garments of skins **and clothed them**"* (Gen. 3:21, emphasis mine).

Adam and Eve tried to cover themselves by sewing leaves from a tree. How unreasonable. Today, it is equally tragic for people to rely on their own self-righteousness hoping they are good enough. But *it was the Lord who supplied Adam and Eve with what they needed.* He clothed them in leather cloaks to cover their nakedness. An animal had to be slain to produce these cloaks, which could be considered the first sacrifice. In the same way, the Lord continues to cover sinners who heartily trust Him and understand that the fig leaves of their efforts could never be enough; He clothes them with His own worth, His own perfect righteousness.

As the narration of Genesis progresses, *we increasingly get to know who the True God is and how He saves people,* both from the punishment their sin deserves and from their alienation from Himself. Especially in the story of Abraham, to which we will now turn, we discover a series of encounters Abraham had with a divine person appearing in human form. The Lord whom Abraham saw with his own eyes (Gen. 12.7) is none other than the Lord Jesus, as no human being can see the face of God the Father and live. The Lord Jesus is the sent Lord, the one who has always made God the Father known to men (John 1:18). In His meetings with Abraham, the Lord Jesus presents Himself as the Word of the Lord, the Angel of the Lord, and as the seen LORD/YHWH, the one who alone reveals the unseen Father.

The story of Abraham

As we study Genesis 12, we mentally travel to the beginning of the second millennium BC. About two thousand years have passed since humanity's catastrophic fall. God elected Abraham from a pagan family (Josh. 24:2) to create the nation of Israel from his descendants. Israel has a unique role to play in God's plan—they will be the recipients and custodians of God's oracles until the promised deliverer is born into this nation. To fulfill God's plan, the Lord Jesus *is seen* by Abraham and gives him His promises (Gen. 12:1-7). These promises concern Abraham's descendant (his singular offspring), and through this seed, these promises extend to all the families of the earth (12:3). Remarkably, God has *always* cared for all nations. From now on, the seed of Genesis 3:15 is sought in the family tree of Abraham.

Jesus, the Word of the Lord

As the story continues, we meet Christ again in Genesis 15, and this time we see Him called *the Word of the Lord*. The same person is also named "the Lord" (YHWH) by the text in 15:7-8. With this title, "the Word of the Lord," Jesus Christ appears in various other parts of the OT as well. For example, in 1 Samuel 3, the Word of the Lord *stood* and called young Samuel (3:1, 10, 21). Moreover, in Jeremiah, we read that *"the word of the Lord"* came to Jeremiah and spoke to him (1:4). In fact, the same person who spoke with Jeremiah is called "Lord" a little later as we read that the Lord *put forth His hand and touched* Jeremiah's mouth (1:9). This description should not be explained away as mere anthropomorphism. It is best to conclude that the Word of the Lord appeared to Jeremiah in human form.

In the Hebrew OT text, we often find the expression "the word of the Lord came to such and such, saying ...." In several of these instances, this phrase refers to a Divine Person, the Word (Jonah 1:1; Jeremiah 1:4, 13; Ezekiel 1:3, 6:1; Zechariah 4:8-9; etc.). It is the Word, then, the second person of the Trinity, who always comes to the prophets and reveals to them the will and character of God the Father. The OT revelation of Christ as the Word of God is the foundation upon which the evangelist John bases his words when he speaks of the eternal Word (Logos) who was with God from the beginning and was God Himself (John 1:1-18).

Abraham's meeting with the Word is described as follows: *"After these things the word of the LORD* **came** *to Abram in a* **vision:** *'Fear not, Abram, I am your shield; your reward shall be very great'"* (Gen. 15:1, emphasis mine). The Word of the Lord *appears* in a vision to Abraham and again gives him His promises; these promises do not depend on Abraham's efforts but only on the goodness of the Lord. The result? We read that *"[Abram] believed the LORD; and he counted it to him as righteousness"* (Gen. 15:6).

Abraham believed in the Lord Jesus, the Word; he accepted His promises, which concerned the descendant that OT believers expected to come. And Genesis tells us that his faith was counted to him as righteousness. All this took place before Abraham was circumcised, which happens later, in Genesis 17. *There is no need, then, for any ceremony or any other human work for man to be saved.* The apostle Paul constantly taught that *sinful man is saved by grace alone, through faith alone in Jesus Christ.* To prove that his teaching is not original but is exactly the same truth that we find in Genesis, Paul used this incident from Abraham's life. (See Romans 3 & 4; Galatians 3.) For example, Paul wrote, "*... the Scripture, foreseeing that God would justify the Gentiles **by faith,** preached the **gospel** beforehand to Abraham, saying, 'In you shall all the nations be blessed'*" (Gal. 3:8, emphasis mine).

For Paul, it is clear that Abraham was saved by believing in Christ regardless of his own works and that *the blessing* of Genesis 12, which would come to the nations, *is man's justification by faith only.* It is worth emphasizing *that people have always been saved in the same way—by faith alone in Christ.* No one was ever saved by observing the law or the various ceremonies. Indeed, Abraham believed in the Christ who would come to save His people; he believed in the Divine Messiah, who would be called "the Lord, our righteousness" (Jeremiah 23:5-6). That is why he is called the father of faith. The only way for a sinner to be saved today is to imitate the faith of Abraham, the friend of God, as the Bible calls him (James 2:23).

Dear reader, do you have the same faith as Abraham? Do you have the same humble trust in the Lord Jesus, who becomes our righteousness when we believe in Him (1 Cor. 1:30)?

Jesus, the Angel of the Lord

We saw the Word of the Lord in Genesis 15. In chapter 16, we meet the Lord with another title; we see Him called *"the Angel of the Lord."* The word *"angel"* in both Hebrew and Greek does not necessarily mean an angelic creature, but more generally means *messenger,* or "sent one".

The Lord Jesus is the sent Lord, who reveals the Most High God. Every appearance of this Divine Messenger is a Christophany;[12] we will have the opportunity to study more of them as the story of redemption unfolds.

In Genesis 16:7-14, we see the Angel of the Lord (who is also called Lord-YHWH and God—16:13) caring about Hagar, the slave of Abraham, and pitying her while she is in desperate need. Isn't that what the Lord Jesus does to this day? He does not remain distant, but He is our merciful High Priest who understands us, the Good Shepherd of the sheep. Indeed, Jesus is our "El Roi," the God who sees us; this is how Hagar called Him: *So [Hagar] called the name of the LORD who spoke to her, 'You are a God of seeing [El Roi],' for she said, 'Truly here I have seen him who looks after me'"* (Gen. 16:13). El Roi means "the God who sees me." The more we comprehend through faith that Jesus *sees* us, the more we grasp our deepest and most permanent identity—*we are His beloved* (cf. the apostle John's experience at the foot of the Cross, the disciple whom Jesus loved—John 19:26).

Jesus, the Lord–YHWH, the righteous Judge

In chapter 17:1, we see the Lord *appearing* to Abraham and making known to him another one of His titles—"I am God Almighty" (in Hebrew: El-Shaddai). The Lord Jesus is Almighty; He has all power and authority. Once again, we see Him revealing the attributes of the true God to people. And it could not be otherwise since Jesus is the image of the invisible God.

In chapter 18, *we see the Lord (YHWH) appear in human form to Abraham,* along with two angelic beings. The fact that the Lord Jesus appears in human form is undeniable since we see Him eat in the presence of Abraham (18:8). We could say that *the Lord Jesus expresses His holy impatience.* He eagerly waits for the fullness of time when the Word will take on human flesh. Then the Lord will not merely appear temporarily in human form but become incarnate—He will become like us.

The reason for this visit is twofold: on the one hand, the Lord announces to the now elderly Abraham that his sterile wife Sarah will give birth to a son in a year, the son of promise (since nothing is impossible to the Almighty Lord); on the other, He reveals Himself as *the Judge of all the Earth* (18:25), since He comes to judge Sodom and Gomorrah for their abominable immorality (Ezek. 16:49-50). Surely, the Lord Jesus is the righteous Judge, as the Father has ordained Him to judge the whole world in His second coming. Indeed, the way the Lord destroys the sinful cities of Sodom and Gomorrah in Genesis 19 is but *a small foretaste* of the terrible judgment that will take place at the end of the world when the wrath of the Lamb will be unleashed against His enemies (Rev. 6:12-17).

Another small, shadowy foretaste of the final judgment is Noah's flood (Gen. chs. 6 to 8), as the NT confirms (2 Pet. 2:4-10; Jude 7). At the final judgment, justice will be served; Adam's fell, dead tree with all his descendants will end up where it deserves to be, in a garbage dump, in eternal hell. This is the greatest tragedy, to find oneself in that place where the fire burns without ever being extinguished, and the worm eats away at people's flesh without ever dying. This is what the incarnate Jesus Himself taught in the Gospels. Sometimes people today are reluctant to speak or hear about hell. Nevertheless, *Jesus talked about hell more than anyone else in the Bible.* And this is an act of love so that people may wake up, realize what awaits them, and run to the great Savior while there is still time.

And still, all these terrible judgments give but a tiny picture of the judgment that fell on Christ when He died on the cross, taking upon Himself the punishment we deserve. *There* He suffered the Father's inconceivable, righteous wrath because of our sins so that we might find healing in His wounds. He drank to the fullest the eternal hell we deserve. This is why *the only safe place in the whole world is the cross of Christ* because *there,* God's wrath has already been poured out, and therefore it will never break out *there* again.

Everyone will meet Christ one day: either today, as their Lord and

Savior, if by faith they hide in the shadow of the cross; or that day, in His second coming, as their Judge. But then it will be too late.

That was the case for Sodom and Gomorrah. The Lord's patience with these cities was exhausted. After centuries of patience, the time of judgment had come for them. He first saved Abraham's nephew Lot by His angels (Lot is called righteous in 2 Peter 2 simply because he had the same faith as his uncle Abraham, not because his life was perfect—since it was not). Then, He unleashed His righteous wrath against sinful Sodom and Gomorrah: *"Then **the LORD** rained on Sodom and Gomorrah sulfur and fire **from the LORD** out of heaven"* (Gen. 19:24).

Amazingly, *in Genesis 19:24, we see two divine Persons named "LORD"* (YHWH): the Lord Jesus who is on earth, as He has just conversed face to face with Abraham, and the Lord who is in heaven. Verses like this one demonstrate beyond reasonable doubt that the believing Israelites (such as Moses, who wrote Genesis) knew perfectly well that the true God is not some impersonal, undefined, or unipersonal being. They knew *two* distinct Lords, *the Lord in heaven and the sent Lord*. Furthermore, in other verses, we likewise see the Spirit of the Lord, who is also a divine Person with emotions. For example, in Isaiah 63:7-14, the prophet recounts God's mercy in delivering the Israelites from the bondage of Egypt, and in that passage, we see all three Divine Persons mentioned: the Lord of Heaven, who was afflicted in the afflictions of His people; the Angel of His presence (the Lord Jesus), who redeemed Israel in His love and pity; and the Holy Spirit, who gave rest to the Israelites, and yet they rebelled and grieved Him.

The truth concerning the Trinity was not hidden from OT believers. How could it be otherwise? This is the most fundamental truth about who the true God is—*three Divine Persons united in a perfect, eternal fellowship of love.*

The assertion that OT believers knew and related to the distinct Persons of the Trinity may sound strange today. This confusion could be explained by the widespread tendency to approach the OT expecting to find there a God defined as "the god of monotheism." And then Christ is defined as a "nuance" that must be added to a more fundamental divine reality. But this conception applies to the "god" of Aristotle, not the God of the Bible! If we discard such misconceptions, we too will be able, together with the Christians who lived both before and after the Lord's incarnation, to discern the Triune God in the OT Scriptures.

Indeed, the ancient church and the first apologists used the OT Scriptures to support their claim that Christ is God, that He is the sent YHWH/Lord who became incarnate. Quotations from the writings of various theologians and apologists (both from the time of the early church and from the time of the Reformation onwards) that emphatically express this understanding are presented in the **Appendix.**

Moreover, the works of several ancient Jewish rabbis, which clearly state that two Divine Persons exist in heaven, are preserved to this day (relevant articles are included in the "Suggestions for further reading" section). This is why we do not find any disagreements about the Trinity and the three Divine Persons anywhere in the NT. There wasn't some theological crisis; the believing Jews (the first disciples of Christ were Jews) were not trying somehow to fit the Person of Jesus into their monotheistic conception. It was acknowledged by all that *Jesus is Lord.* And when the apostles called Jesus "Lord," it was clear to everyone that they were not merely claiming that Jesus has a position of equivalence with God; rather, *they identified Jesus with YHWH, the God of Israel.*

The widespread use of the Septuagint[13] while the NT was being composed explains why the title "Lord" was understood to mean that Jesus is the incarnate YHWH. In the Septuagint translation of the Hebrew Bible into Greek, the name "YHWH" (the covenant name of God), was translated as *"Kyrios"* (Lord). When the NT writers quoted the OT, they always chose to translate the name "YHWH" as "Kyrios," following the example of the Septuagint. Indeed, an examination of the NT's usage of the OT affirms the identification of the person of Jesus with the Lord/YHWH (cf. Matt. 3:3 with Isa. 40:3; Phil. 2:10-11 with Isa. 45:23; John 12:41 with Isa. 6:1-5; Rom. 10:13 with Joel 2:32). Since the various Greek-speaking Jewish communities used the

Septuagint extensively, they would not miss the apostles' intent. There-fore, by giving the title "Lord" to Jesus, the apostles declared that He is the Almighty YHWH who became incarnate.

Actually, one of the early church's first confessions of faith was that *"Jesus is Lord."* Short and meaningful. In contrast to Judaism, this con-fession recognizes that Jesus of Nazareth is YHWH, the eternal Lord of hosts. In contradistinction to the faith of the Roman Empire, this confession proclaims that Jesus is the universal and only true Emperor. Paul alludes to this confession in Romans (cf. 1 Cor. 12:3): *"... if you confess with your mouth that **Jesus is Lord** and believe in your heart that God raised him from the dead, you will be saved"* (Rom. 10:9, emphasis mine). Interestingly, Paul goes on to write *"... 'everyone who calls on the name of the **Lord** will be saved'"* (Rom. 10:13, emphasis mine). This statement is a direct quotation from the OT prophet Joel (Joel 2:32), where the name to be called on is "YHWH." Hence, when the apostle Paul confesses that "Jesus is Lord," he does not merely acknowledge Jesus' lordship; he proclaims that *Jesus is the preexistent YHWH in the flesh.* Since most English Bible versions translate God's name YHWH as "LORD" in the OT,[14] I will follow this rendering from now on and refer to Jesus as *LORD,* to stress His divine identity.

The sacrifice of Isaac, a prefiguration of the Cross

One year after the destruction of Sodom and Gomorrah, the child that the LORD had promised to Abraham has miraculously been conceived and brought into the world by Sarah. The years go by and Isaac, Abra-ham's son, is now a teenager. At this point in time, *in chapter 22 of Genesis, we come across the well-known story of Isaac's sacrifice.* Why is this story here? For some people, this story is a challenge to their faith. Can God ask Abraham to sacrifice his own son? What is the point of all this?

And yet, when this story is rightly understood (like every passage of Scripture), we see the LORD Jesus more clearly, and our faith in Him is strengthened. We read this story correctly when we see it in relation to what has preceded it. Abraham waits for the offspring who will crush the serpent's head. Indeed, the LORD has revealed to him that this descendant will come from the genealogical line of his son Isaac, the promised child (Gen. 15:4, 21:12). So, when the LORD asks Abraham to offer his beloved son as a burnt offering, this is a test of faith. Yet, God is not making any random request to test Abraham's faith in general. He leads him through this process to test Abraham's confidence in the specific promise that the descendant will come from Isaac. Abraham trusts in the LORD and His promise about Isaac. So he obeys without delay. The next day, early in the morning, he begins the journey toward the place the LORD has indicated to him. He does not hesitate to sacrifice Isaac, knowing that the LORD is trustworthy. As we see in Hebrews 11:17-19, Abraham pondered that the LORD would certainly fulfill His promise, and so he expected that the LORD, after the sacrifice, would resurrect Isaac from the dead.

Undeniably, the story's progression displays the LORD's *faithfulness,* as He intervenes and does not let Abraham complete the sacrifice of his son. Never again will the LORD ask for such a thing, and indeed, human sacrifices will be explicitly forbidden by the law that God will give to Moses. What is the point of all this, then? The goal for Abraham was to grow in his knowledge of the LORD. The same is true for everyone studying this story. *As a matter of fact, in this story (and throughout the OT), the LORD Jesus manifests Himself in the following ways:*

- He is really, visibly, present. The LORD Jesus appears as the Angel of the LORD, who is also called "LORD" (Gen. 22:15; cf. 22:1 with 22:11-12)
- He manifests Himself through the promises/prophecies given for the work the promised offspring will do to defeat the enemies of His people (Gen. 22:17-18)
- He manifests Himself as the object of Abraham's (and every other believer's) faith

- He manifests Himself through the *typology*, that is, the *symbolism* of the story.

Regarding the symbolism of this story, we observe the following about how the LORD manifests Himself:

God asks Abraham to go to the land of Moriah (Gen. 22:2) and sacrifice Isaac, "his only son" (while Abraham has other children, Isaac is called his only son, which is no coincidence). And this location is mentioned once more in 2 Chronicles 3:1, where we learn that on Mount Moriah (where the sacrifice was to be made), centuries later, Jerusalem was to be built.

Furthermore, let us note that when Isaac, who was old enough to carry the wood for the sacrifice, asks his father where the lamb for the sacrifice is (22:7), Abraham replies, "God will provide." Finally, after the LORD stops Abraham from sacrificing his son, He provides not a lamb but a ram. This is why Abraham called that place *Yahweh Jireh,* which means *"the LORD will provide."* Moses writes, *"So Abraham called the name of that place, 'The LORD will provide'; as it is said to this day, 'On the mount of the LORD it shall be provided'"* (Gen. 22:14).

Abraham knew that on that specific mountain, which is the location of future Jerusalem, the LORD would provide the lamb of sacrifice. And Moses, who wrote Genesis around 1500 BC, about five hundred years after these events took place, points out that then, so many years later, the Israelites continued to say that "on the mount of the LORD it shall be *provided.*"

Truly, what Abraham faithfully expected to happen took place. About two thousand years later, on that same mountain, God the Father held *His only begotten Son* by the hand and led Him to Calvary. And then there was no one to stop this sacrifice. The Father *provided* the Lamb, as the LORD Jesus voluntarily offered Himself as a burnt offering on the Cross (metaphorically speaking, as He took upon Himself the fiery wrath of God because of our sins).

Dear reader, look again at this story. *Who do you see now?* Do you perceive the One who did not spare *His only begotten Son,* but delivered Him for us all? Do you see the One who provided for our greatest need, giving what was most precious to Him? Do you foresee the Lamb of God who takes away the sin of the world? As the apostle Paul so beautifully writes, *"He who did not spare his own Son but gave him up for us all, how will he not also with him graciously give us all things?"* (Rom. 8:32).

Why are we given the stories of Genesis?

By examining Genesis with the Christ-centered interpretive key that the LORD Himself and His apostles have given us, we comprehend that all these Bible stories focus on a divine Person. By learning His titles as we study Genesis, we are better prepared to identify Jesus throughout the OT Scriptures and learn many aspects of the LORD's character.

The story of Abraham, specifically, enables us to know the LORD Jesus as the one who sees us, is Almighty, and cares about everything in our lives. He cares, for He is the Lamb of God who was slain on the cross so that whoever heartily trusts in Him may find forgiveness and eternal life. Let us trust Him, then, and live by daily looking to Yahweh Jireh, the LORD who provides.

* * *

The story goes on, and the same promises are given to *Isaac,* to whom the LORD Jesus also manifests Himself (Gen. 26:1-4, 24). Then the LORD Jesus reveals Himself to Isaac's son, Jacob.

The story of Jacob

Jacob is an ungodly man—he deceives his father and takes the name of the LORD in vain (27:20). The result of his deception was to steal the blessing reserved for his elder brother. Fearing for his life, Jacob is forced to abandon his father's house and go live with his uncle Laban.

During his journey, Jacob came to a certain place and stayed there all night, because the sun had set. He was lonely, destitute, and so tired that he took one of the stones of that place and put it at his head, and he lay down in that place to sleep. He feels far away from God, unfit to reach up to Him. But the LORD is with Jacob, and *He* will reach down to him. We read that *"... [Jacob] dreamed, and behold, there was a ladder set up on the earth, and the top of it reached to heaven. And behold, **the angels of God were ascending and descending on it**"* (Gen. 28:12, emphasis mine).

Incredibly, Jacob receives the same *promises* as his father and grandfather: *"And behold, the LORD stood above [the ladder] and said, 'I am the LORD, the God of Abraham your father and the God of Isaac. The land on which you lie **I will give to you and to your offspring.** Your offspring shall be like the dust of the earth, and you shall spread abroad to the west and to the east and to the north and to the south, and **in you and your offspring shall all the families of the earth be blessed**'"* (Gen. 28:13-14, emphasis mine). So heaven's stairway is not built by our efforts but by God's *promise* to come down in Christ to rescue us.

In this vision, the LORD *Jesus* stood on a stairway; this stairway was set up on the earth, and the top of it reached to heaven. This vision is a picture of Jesus, who comes to bridge the enormous gap between heaven and earth. Indeed, 1,800 years after these events took place the incarnate LORD stated, *"Truly, truly, I say to you, you will see heaven opened, and **the angels of God ascending and descending on the Son of Man**"* (John 1:51, emphasis mine). Indeed, Jesus *is* our stairway to heaven and, thus, Christians always stand at the gate of heaven. So, Christian, if you find yourself in a bad place like Jacob, remember that Jesus is right there with you!

We know that the LORD who appeared to Jacob was the LORD *Jesus, the Angel,* because Genesis clarifies it later on. As the years go by, Jacob works for his uncle Laban. He works for about twenty years to marry Rachel and Leah, Laban's daughters (chs. 29 & 30), at which point he decides to leave from there. Then, he informs Rachel and Leah that *"the angel of God, the God of Bethel,"* told him to go back to the land of his kindred (31:9-13).

Having chosen to return home, Jacob will have to meet his brother Esau, whom he has deceived, and therefore he is afraid of what may happen. That very night, while Jacob was alone, a man wrestled with him until daybreak (32:23-32). As the narrator says, *"[this man] touched his hip socket, and Jacob's hip was put out of joint as he wrestled with him"* (32:25). This night, Jacob sees the LORD Jesus face to face. Indeed, Jacob's opponent was no ordinary man. We know that Jacob wrestled with God Himself in visible form that night since we read, *"… Jacob was left alone. And a man wrestled with him until the breaking of the day. … So Jacob called the name of the place Peniel, saying, 'For **I have seen God face to face**, and yet my life has been delivered'"* (Gen. 32:24, 30, emphasis mine).

In Hosea 12:1-6, we find further corroboration that the One with whom Jacob strove is *God, the Angel, the LORD*. The prophet Hosea, who lived many hundreds of years later, takes the identity of this Person for granted.

Why is the story of Jacob's wrestle with Christ included in the Bible? The goal is for us to see how the LORD Jesus acts to save Jacob. Until then, Jacob was a man who had confidence in himself, his deceptions, and his efforts. This night, however, he has reached his limits; he understands he cannot succeed on his own. Perhaps this is the first moment in his life that he truly trusts in the LORD. This is why the narration tells us that Jacob prevailed (Hosea 12:4). He prevailed, for as prophet Hosea writes, *"… [Jacob] wept and sought his favor."* In this passage, Hosea calls on the Israelites to return to the living God, whom they have repeatedly forsaken. So, Hosea is telling them—Go back to your God, just as Jacob did.

What about you, dear reader? Where and whom do you trust? Like Jacob, are you ready to say to the LORD, "I will not let you go unless you bless me"? (Gen. 32:26b).

We have seen that Abraham knew the LORD in heaven and the

Angel, the sent/seen LORD. Jacob had the same knowledge (as evidenced by his prayer to the Angel, his Redeemer—Gen. 48:3, 15-16). This knowledge of the Triune God is transmitted, from generation to generation, by the genealogical line from which the LORD will become incarnate to crush the snake's head, as He had promised to do from the very beginning (Gen. 3:15).

The story of Joseph

The story continues with the next generation, Joseph, the son of Jacob (chs. 37 to 50). The LORD continues to direct all things according to His wise plan. Part of God's plan is for Joseph to be sold by his brothers as a slave and end up in Egypt (Ps. 105:17). Indeed, Joseph's brothers envied him so much that they sold him into slavery to some Midianite traders passing by who were on their way to Egypt.

Joseph knows the LORD is sovereign over all things, so he keeps trusting in Him. Christ has not forgotten His servant; Genesis repeatedly tells us He is with him, even in prison (Gen. 39:2, 21). A slave and facing unjust charges, Joseph remains imprisoned for more than ten years. But even then, he trusts that the LORD who led him to such a grueling situation will stay with him and eventually set him free. Indeed, in the fullness of time, the LORD exalts Joseph and places him second in command. Joseph, by now vindicated and free of bitterness, tells his brothers when they come to Egypt, *"As for you, **you meant evil against me, but God meant it for good,** to bring it about that many people should be kept alive, as they are today"* (Gen. 50:20, emphasis mine).

Here is God's plan: Joseph experiences humiliation, injustice, pain, and sorrow; even death, metaphorically speaking, as he is thrown into a pit. But that's not the end—he is lifted up to Pharaoh's right hand, and, with the wisdom the LORD gives him, Joseph saves his family and all of Egypt from the terrible famine that had fallen over all the earth at that time. Joseph's brothers meant evil against him when they sold him into slavery; God meant the same event for good.

The shape of Joseph's life can be depicted as a V: the first part moves downwards to the pit of despair and then rises to the right of Pharaoh to save the people from starvation. This shape resembles the shape of the incarnate LORD's life: from heaven's glory to the humiliation of the incarnation, as He added our own human nature to His divine hypostasis. This humiliation continued throughout His lowly life as He faced endless temptations, derisions, an unfair trial, scourging, the crown of thorns, the beatings, the nails, and finally, the horrible crucifixion, as He died bearing the sins of His Church to save her from eternal hell. And then, after the cross comes the endless glory, as the resurrected and triumphant LORD Jesus is seated at the Father's right hand (Phil. 2:1-11).

In the story of Joseph's life, the supreme omnipotence of the LORD Jesus is clearly seen. *He is truly the Lord of human history and of every human life.* The LORD's miraculous providence, which so shines through the story of Joseph, fills His own people with joy and peace. Anyone who refuses to accept that God is truly Sovereign, namely that the LORD controls all things meticulously, ends up with a distorted image of God. As a result, such a person deprives himself of *the steadfast anchor—an unreserved trust in the LORD and His sovereign love for His own.*

* * *

At this point, we reach the end of the OT's first book. Jacob and all his descendants have migrated to Egypt. The LORD had foretold to Abraham what would happen to his descendants: *"Then the LORD said to Abram, 'Know for certain that your offspring will be sojourners in a land that is not theirs and will be servants there, and **they will be afflicted for four hundred years'"** (Gen. 15:13). This prophecy was given to Jacob's grandfather centuries ago. Now the time is ready for its fulfillment.

And so, the LORD's plan continues in the book of Exodus. The exodus (mass departure) of Jacob's descendants (the *Israelites,* as the

LORD had renamed Jacob to Israel) from the slavery of Egypt *is the greatest paradigmatic redemption event in the OT* (Exod. 6:6). This event defines all subsequent generations, so they repeatedly refer to it (e.g., 1 Sam. 12; 1 Kings 8; Job 19:25; Ps. 29, 77, 78, 106; Isa. 43, 63; Mich. 6:4). Let us turn our attention there.

The Story of the Exodus from Egypt: The LORD Jesus takes His people out of the land of slavery to worship God

Many years after Joseph's death, a new Pharaoh, who does not know him, comes to power. And because the Egyptians were afraid of the Israelites, who had multiplied in the meantime, Pharaoh enslaved them to forced labor. When this plan proved to be ineffective, he commanded the midwives to kill the male babies of the Israelites the moment they were born. Because they refused to obey him, Pharaoh causes the blame for these atrocities to fall upon all Egyptians; thus, from now on they are all guilty: *"Then Pharaoh* **commanded all his people,** *'Every son that is born to the Hebrews you shall cast into the Nile, but you shall let every daughter live'"* (Exod. 1:22).

In Exodus chapter 3, we see the Angel of the LORD speaking with Moses (Exod. 3:2). *This Angel is also called the God of Abraham, of Isaac, and Jacob (3:6), the great I AM* (Exod. 3:14-15), *the LORD* [YHWH] (3:4). The LORD has chosen Moses as the leader to deliver His people from slavery. The LORD Jesus then addresses the eighty-year-old Moses out of the burning bush with what can be described as the *summary* of the book of Exodus: "[God] said, 'But I will be with you, and this shall be the sign for you, that I have sent you: when you have brought the people out of Egypt, you shall serve God on this mountain'" (Exod. 3:12).

Moses, the burning bush, and the LORD Jesus

It is worth focusing on the way Moses described this encounter. He was an eyewitness; thus, he recorded his own experience. He tells us that the Angel of the LORD appeared to him out of the midst of a burning bush (3:2); he immediately adds that the LORD was in the midst of the burning bush. These are not two different persons. *The Angel of the LORD is the LORD. He is the sent LORD, the LORD from the LORD* (as the Nicene Creed states: Light of Light, very God of very God). Then, the LORD Jesus, as Moses writes, makes the following astounding statement about Himself, *"'I am the God of your father, the God of Abraham, the God of Isaac, and the God of Jacob.' And Moses hid his face, for he was afraid* **to look at God***"* (Exod. 3:6, emphasis mine).

Some may say, "Show us where Jesus claimed to be God." In Exodus 3:6, *Jesus proclaims that He is the God of Abraham, Isaac, and Jacob.* Muslims and modern Jews delude themselves into thinking that they believe in the God of Abraham. They are deceived, for the God of Abraham *is* the LORD Jesus, whom they deny. Jehovah's Witnesses deny the Divinity of the LORD Jesus; the OT rebukes them.

Moses, who discerns the sent LORD, wants his readers to know Him also. He wants to turn our attention to the one who proclaims to be the *"I AM WHO I AM"* (3:14).

So, let us turn to Him. It is worth noting that during Moses' conversation with the LORD, Jesus stands in the burning bush, in the fire. And in this symbolic way (fire symbolizes suffering) the LORD shows His identification with His people. He has heard their cry, He has seen their afflictions, He knows their sufferings (3:7). And He does not stay away but descends to be with them. He enters with them into the furnace of affliction (just as the LORD Jesus did with the "three children in the furnace"—Dan. 3:24-28). The burning bush is a spectacular type of the LORD's care for His *spiritual* people today—for those who believe in Him. He isn't distant today either, but by His Spirit, He is closer to us than we can perceive. He isn't indifferent to our pain, but He sympathizes with us, as He has become our merciful High Priest. And above all, He entered the furnace by descending into the fire of hell on the cross. He did it for us, to save us from the most horrible slavery, the most terrible future. He redeemed us by dying, without being destroyed Himself, as He conquered death by His resurrection.

Christian, the LORD is with you whether you feel it or not. He has borne your pains and carried your sorrows on the cross (Isa. 53). He understands you, and He cares. Therefore, He promises that when (when, *not* if) you pass through the waters, they shall not overwhelm you, and when you walk through fire, you shall not be burned, for the LORD, your Redeemer, will be with you (Isa. 43:1-3). He does not promise a life without problems; this must wait for the new heavens and the new earth. However, what He promises is His protection and care amid troubles. So don't think that Christ has forgotten you or that He is indifferent to what you go through. Instead, when found in the furnace of trials, turn to Him. Oftentimes, you will experience His presence in an intense and personal way. But even if the clouds keep hiding His face, you may be confident that underneath it all "are the everlasting arms" (Deut. 33:27).

* * *

Back to our narration. The LORD Jesus, the second Person of the Trinity, hears the cry of the Israelites, is with them, and acts to lead the people to Mount Sinai, where they will worship God the Father—the first Person of the Trinity (Exod. 3:12: *God will lead His people to God;* this is indeed the *summary* of Exodus). The LORD sends plague after plague against the Egyptians to force Pharaoh let His people go (Exod. 7 to 12).

But the Israelites were just as sinful as the Egyptians since they also worshiped the idols of the Egyptians (Josh. 24:14). So, to save His people from the devastating judgment that the LORD Himself will bring against the Egyptians (11:4-5), someone must pay for the Israelites; there must be a substitutionary sacrifice. This happens at Passover (the Hebrew word *Passover/Pesach* means to *"pass over"* and refers to both the feast and the animal that would be sacrificed—see Exod. 12). The Israelite families are covered by the blood of a lamb without blemish. The LORD has ordered every family to slaughter such a lamb and put its blood on the two doorposts and the lintel of their homes. Thus, when the destroyer comes that night to kill the firstborns of the Egyptians, *He passes over* ("Passover") the doors smeared with the blood of the lamb. *The events of Passover are the tenth plague.* The same event that is judgment for the Egyptians, is salvation for the Israelites.

The significance of the Passover story

Through the story of the night of the exodus, God intends to show to all with eyes to see two surprising truths:

1. Salvation comes through judgment
2. Salvation comes thanks to a substitutionary sacrifice (one must die in the place of another).

Indeed, that night every house had an individual who died. *In the homes of the Egyptians, their firstborn son was killed.* (This was a just punishment. Let us recall that all Egyptians participated in the killing of the male babies of the Israelites; moreover, the LORD had warned Pharaoh that if he refused to let Israel—God's firstborn son—go, the LORD would kill Pharaoh's firstborn son—Exod. 4:22-23.) *In the homes of the Israelites, the lamb was killed instead.*

The events of Passover *point* to the final, perfect sacrifice of the Lamb of God as follows. We, also, are guilty like the Israelites. Therefore, we are under the judgment that will occur when the LORD Jesus, the righteous Judge, returns from heaven (John 5:22; Acts 17:31). For us to be saved from the coming judgment (or better, through the coming judgment), someone had to die in our place; someone who is perfect and blameless: *the Lamb of God,* the LORD Jesus (John 1:29).

Some, of course, refuse to recognize their guilt. They think that they are "good enough" and that God is obligated to forgive their little "mistakes" (so they say, man's ability to delude himself is inexhaustible). Contrary to such outlandish perceptions, we have seen the Bible's verdict—we are born both guilty and corrupt. The simple proof? All I have to do is examine myself in the mirror of God's law, in the mirror of the Ten Commandments, to find out what my condition is before God. I will then realize that I am guilty of idolatry (every time I love something or someone more than God, I become an idolater), I am a liar, and I covet the things of my neighbor (the tenth commandment, which goes deeper than any human law, examines the heart of man: *"You shall not covet your neighbor's house; you shall not covet your neighbor's wife … or anything that is your neighbor's"* – Exod. 20:17). Anyone who honestly examines himself must admit that he has transgressed all ten commandments.

Still, some may say, "This isn't true of me. I have neither committed murder nor adultery (Exod. 20:13-14)." Such people should carefully consider how the LORD Jesus expounded the deeper meaning of the Law in the sermon of the Mount: *"You have heard that it was said to those of old, 'You shall not murder; and whoever murders will be liable to judgment.' But I say to you that everyone who is angry with his brother will be liable to judgment; whoever insults his brother will be liable to the council; and whoever says, 'You fool!' will be liable to the hell of fire. … You have heard that it was said, 'You shall not commit adultery.' But I say to you that everyone who looks at a woman with lustful intent has already committed adultery with her in his heart"* (Matt. 5:21-22, 27-28). The words of Jesus expose our sinfulness to the Law's condemnation. *The verdict is: Guilty. Indeed, guilty of cosmic treason.*

How can one be saved? The answer is prefigured by the Passover events—whoever is covered by the blood of Christ will be redeemed and thus spared from the wrath of God that will be unleashed on judgment day (1 Pet. 1:18-19). For *Christ is our Passover lamb,* who has been sacrificed for us (1 Cor. 5:7). Judgment fell upon Christ on the cross so that those who believe in Him would pass safely with the LORD Jesus through the fire of judgment, solely because of His own sacrifice in our place. This is why the apostle Paul's words in Romans 8:1 apply to all those who are in Christ: *"There is therefore now **no condemnation** for those who are in Christ Jesus"* (emphasis mine). To be in Christ is to be united with Him through faith and, thus, safely hidden in Jesus, free of all condemnation.

Everyone who is washed in the blood will be saved. But how can the precious blood of the Lamb cover someone? The hyssop's *typology* provides a visual explanation. Let us focus, then, on the narration of the Passover night:

> *"Then Moses called all the elders of Israel and said to them, 'Go and select lambs for yourselves according to your clans, and kill the Passover lamb. Take a bunch of hyssop and dip it in the blood that is in the basin, and touch the lintel and the two doorposts with the blood that is in the basin. None of you shall go out of the door of his house until the morning. For the LORD will pass through to strike the Egyptians, and when he sees the blood on the lintel and on the two doorposts, the LORD will pass over the door and will not allow the destroyer to enter your houses to strike you.'"* (Exod. 12:21-23)

Moses asked the Israelites to trust the word of the LORD and obey it (he himself followed his own advice—see Heb. 11:28). They had to collect the blood of the slaughtered lamb and, dipping in the blood a bunch of hyssop (a simple, ordinary plant), touch the door of their house with the blood-soaked hyssop bunch. He did not ask them to use gold or precious stones, but a simple, humble bunch of an ordinary plant. The point is that *what is important is not the bunch* with which the Israelites applied the animal's blood to the doors *but the very blood* of the slaughtered lamb. *The way we cover ourselves with the blood of the Lamb of God, with the shed blood of Christ on the cross, is by faith/trust in Him and His priceless sacrifice.* Our faith has no value in itself. All merit exists in the blood of the slaughtered Lamb. *Genuine faith is the bunch of hyssop that applies the blood of Christ.* It is His blood that saves, forgives, cleanses, and sanctifies. Strictly speaking, our faith does not save us. We are saved by Christ, whom we receive through faith (John 1:12). So let no one say, "I must have *strong* faith to be saved." For, again, what saves is not faith per se but the *object* of faith.

D. A. Carson gave a memorable illustration of the perfect sufficiency of Jesus' blood.[15] It is presented here somewhat paraphrased. Think of the scene the day before the first Passover. Two Israelite families, whose houses are side by side, heard the words of Moses and put them in practice—they smeared the two doorposts with the blood of the slaughtered lamb and put blood on the lintel. Both will stay inside their home during the night. As they talk to each other, one family man says to the other:

"Aren't you a little nervous about what's going to happen tonight?"

"Why are you worried? Haven't you heard what the LORD said to Moses? When the LORD comes to the city, He will see the blood on the door and pass over your home."

"Yes, that's how it is, but see how many plagues have come, how much destruction has happened? I put the blood there. But it's pretty scary. How can we be sure of what will happen tonight?"

"Bring it on. I trust the promises of God."

Which one lost his son that night? The answer is neither, for the difference is not in the intensity or clarity of the faith exercised but on the ground of the blood of the lamb. The LORD did not enter their houses to judge whether the Israelites were good enough (there are no such people). The LORD saw the blood at the doorposts and passed over. This is what He had declared to Moses so that he would pass it on to the Israelites: *"The blood shall be a sign for you, on the houses where you are. And **when I see the blood, I will pass over you,** and no plague will befall you to destroy you, when I strike the land of Egypt"* (Exod. 12:13).

We overcome the accuser on the ground of the blood of the Lamb (Rev. 12:11). So, dear reader, do not trust anywhere else except in the LORD Jesus and His shed blood. Those who say they believe in Jesus but simultaneously keep trusting in their works end up *diluting* the blood of the Lamb with water.

Jesus, the Great Warrior

Then, the LORD Jesus accomplishes what he has said to Moses. Pharaoh is forced to let the Israelites go after the tenth plague hits Egypt. And the LORD Jesus is the One who leads the Israelites to Mount Sinai, to God. The Angel of God leads the people through the cloud during the day and through the column of fire during the night. *He, the Angel LORD, fights on behalf of His people* and destroys all their enemies with just one look (Cf. Exod. 13:20-14:1, 14:18-31).

People sometimes have an exceedingly small, inadequate picture of who the LORD Jesus really is. But let us look at a spectacular *title* that Moses and the Israelites attributed to Him. They witnessed the LORD passing them through the Red Sea and destroying the Egyptians' army, so they now praise Him with these words:

> *"The LORD is a man of war;*
> *the LORD is his name."* (Exod. 15:3)

In fact, this is not the only time we meet the LORD fighting and appearing as a Warrior. In Joshua of Nun, after the next generation of the Israelites have passed through the river Jordan and have begun to conquer the land that the LORD had promised them, we read of the following encounter. Joshua, having now succeeded Moses as the people's leader, is near the city of Jericho, probably looking for some weak point of defense. And at that moment, a man with his drawn sword in his hand appears to him (Josh. 5:13 – 6:2). *He is the commander of the army of the LORD.* This commander is undoubtedly the *LORD Jesus,* who, at the right time, comes to fight on behalf of His people. We know this because He tells Joshua that *"the place where you are standing is holy"* (cf. Josh. 5:15 with Exod. 3:5), and also because *the text calls Him LORD* in Joshua 6:2. (We should always remember that the divisions of chapters and verses are not part of the original text; the story continues from chapter 5 to chapter 6 without interruption.)

Truly, just as the LORD crushed Pharaoh's army and all the other enemies of Israel, so now, by His crucifixion and resurrection, the LORD Jesus has crushed the devil (the ancient serpent), along with death, the world, sin, and the flesh. *The LORD Jesus is the great Warrior* (Rev. 19:11-16). He is the triumphant Conqueror, on behalf of and for the sake of all who trust in Him. He is the One who stopped at nothing to fulfill His mission. *He passed through hellfire on the cross in order to save His heart's elect, the Church.*

The meeting with the Most High God on Mount Sinai

In Exodus 19, the Israelites reached *Mount Sinai* after a few months' journey. There, the LORD Jesus said: *"… the LORD said to Moses, 'Go to the people and consecrate them today and tomorrow, and let them wash their garments and be ready for the third day. For on the third day the LORD will come down on Mount Sinai in the sight of all the people'"* (Exod. 19:10-11).

The LORD (the Son) informs Moses that the LORD (the Father) will descend on the top of the mountain in three days. *For the first time in the Bible,* we see God the Father coming into direct contact with human beings.[16] For that to happen, Jesus brought His people to the Father. When the three days pass, havoc ensues—smoke, fire, trumpet blasts, an earthquake, and thunder (Exod. 19:18-19).

At that point, the LORD Jesus asks Moses to warn the people and the priests not to cross the limits set, for otherwise the LORD will break out against them: *"And the LORD said to [Moses], 'Go down, and come up bringing Aaron with you. But do not let the priests and the people break through to come up to the LORD, lest he break out against them'"* (Exod. 19:24).

Once again, we see the Son speaking about something the Father will do. So, Moses went down to the people and, obeying the LORD's command, told them what he heard.

What follows is the oral delivery of the Ten Commandments (ch. 20) by God. All the Israelites saw the thunder and the flashes of lightning, heard the voice of God, and were terrified. They stood far off while Moses entered into the *cloud* to speak with God the Father (20:18-21). *He is covered by the cloud, for in our present state no one can see the face of the Father and continue to live.* Indeed, Moses' encounter with the LORD, whose face he cannot see, was quite different than his encounters with the LORD in the tabernacle, with whom he spoke face-to-face, as he records (33:11). During this meeting, God the Father (or, as He is often called in the OT, the "Most High God"—see Gen. 14:18) says to Moses:

> *"'Behold, I send an **angel** before you to guard you on the way and to bring you to the place that I have prepared. Pay careful attention to him and obey his voice; do not rebel against him, for he will not pardon your transgression, **for my name is in him.** But if you carefully obey his voice and do all that I say, then I will be an enemy to your enemies and an adversary to your adversaries. When **my angel** goes before you and brings you to the Amorites and the Hittites and the Perizzites and the Canaanites, the Hivites and the Jebusites, and I blot them out, you shall not bow down to their gods nor serve them, nor do as they do, but you shall utterly overthrow them and break their pillars in pieces. You shall serve the LORD your God, and he will bless your bread and your water, and **I will take sickness away** from among you."* (Exod. 23:20-25, emphasis mine)

The *Angel* whom the Father will send *has the authority to forgive sins and thus must be God also,* since God alone can forgive sins. This Angel's divinity is clearly implied by the fact that "the name of the LORD is in him" (cf. Mark 2:7; John 14:10). Matthew Henry's Commentary on this passage states that "Christ is the Angel of Jehovah; this is plainly taught by St. Paul, 1 Cor. 10:9."

Then, looking closely at chapter 24, we find that *Moses has two different encounters with two distinct Divine Persons.* In chapter 19, the LORD told Moses that no one but himself should approach the mountain. But in chapter 24, Moses, Aaron, Nadab, Abihu, and seventy of the elders *"saw the God of Israel"* and ate in His presence (Exod. 24:9-11). This is the first meeting. Of course, the LORD whose face people can see is the LORD Jesus.

And then Moses ascends even higher up the mountain, according to the commandment of the LORD. This is the second encounter where this time, having left the elders behind, Moses is alone (only Joshua was with him)—24:12-18. On the top of the mountain, the Father has descended, whose face no one can see (John 1:18). So once again, Moses enters into the cloud.

There, Moses receives detailed instructions for the ark of the Covenant, the tabernacle, etc. He also receives the ten commandments, written by the finger of God (31:18).

Moses remained on the mountain for forty days. During this period, the Israelites commit idolatry (ch. 32). Indeed, when the people of Israel made a molded calf in a vain effort to represent by it the LORD and worshiped it and sacrificed to it, they broke the second commandment. When Moses descends and sees Israel's failure to keep God's Decalogue, he breaks the plates with the ten commandments. Then, he ascends once again to the top of the mountain to intercede on behalf of the people. (Moses' intercession serves as another prefiguration of Christ, the perfect Mediator between God and men.) In chapter 33, Moses converses with the Father once more. The LORD tells him He will not go up among them, lest He consumes them on the way, for they are a stiff-necked people (Exod. 33:3).

Upon hearing these words, Moses said to the LORD, *"'See, you say to me, 'Bring up this people,' but you have not let me know whom you will send with me. Yet you have said, 'I know you by name, and you have also found favor in my sight.' Now therefore, if I have found favor in your sight, please show me now your ways, that I may know you in order to find favor in your sight. Consider too that this nation is your people.' And he* said, *'My presence will go with you, and I will give you rest.'* And he said to him, *'If your presence will not go with me, do not bring us up from here'"* (Exod. 33:12-15, emphasis mine).

Moses knows that he desperately needs God's presence and help. That's why he insists that "God's presence" must go with him during the journey to the promised land. *The presence of God the Father is the LORD Jesus*—The Angel of His Presence (Isaiah 63:9). Thus, Moses essentially says, "Send Jesus to be with us, or we perish."

He then asks to see the glory of the LORD with whom he converses at the top of the mountain, that is, the glory of God the Father (33:18). But no one can see the face of God the Father and live (33:20-23). This is why God first hides Moses in the cleft of the rock and covers him with His hand (so that he may see His back and not His face), and He then passes before him and proclaims the name of the LORD:

> *"The LORD descended in the cloud and stood with him there, and **proclaimed the name of the LORD**. The LORD passed before him and proclaimed, 'The LORD, the LORD, a God merciful and gracious, slow to anger, and abounding in steadfast love and faithfulness, keeping steadfast love for thousands, forgiving iniquity and transgression and sin, but who will by no means clear the guilty, visiting the iniquity of the fathers on the children and the children's children, to the third and the fourth generation.'"* (Exod. 34:5-7, emphasis mine)

When Moses hears God Most High proclaim His essential goodness (which is His glory) with these words (cf. with Exod. 33:19), he recognizes the character of the Angel (23:21). So he asks the Father to send the LORD Jesus with them: *"And Moses quickly bowed his head toward the earth and worshiped. And he said, 'If now I have found favor in your sight, O Lord, **please let the Lord go in the midst of us,** for it is a stiff-necked people, and pardon our iniquity and our sin, and take us for your inheritance'"* (Exod. 34:8-9, emphasis mine).

And truly, the LORD Jesus accompanies the Israelites through the wilderness and into the promised land. He is the One who manifests Himself in the tabernacle and later in the temple of Solomon. It is He who reveals the Most High God to the prophets. He is the God of Israel, the mighty Deliverer, and the Redeeming LORD.

The spiritual significance of the Israelites' Exodus

The recounting of the events of the Israelites' Exodus is designed to display who the LORD is and how He freed His people out of the land of slavery. Similarly, the rest of the Pentateuch shows how He led them through the wilderness to the promised land. This is how the believing Israelites read the Pentateuch, which began to be handed down to them on Mount Sinai. They knew that God is not an impersonal or unipersonal being. They knew the LORD (Jesus) with whom Moses conversed face-to-face, and the LORD that no one can see, who reveals Himself through the sent LORD.

The believing Israelites had as the "entry point" into the Bible's first five books the knowledge of the Exodus events and of the God who revealed Himself to them through these events. With this knowledge as a foundation, they began to study the Pentateuch. And thus, they didn't mistakenly think that God is a unipersonal being; instead, they were able to discern the sent LORD, who revealed to them the Most High God. *We also, today, should have the same expectations as we study the OT.* We should have the correct mental image of God in our minds. Otherwise, the truth of the OT Scriptures will remain largely hidden from our eyes.

The believing Israelites expectantly searched the Scriptures to find out what the coming Messiah would be like and how He would redeem them. They did not trust in their law-keeping. They trusted in the LORD Jesus and waited for Him to fulfill His marvelous promises. Indeed, the LORD Jesus came at the fullness of time, when the Father *redeemed* His people by supplying Christ as a lamb without blemish and without spot (1 Pet. 1:18-19). Thanks solely to the slain and risen

Lamb, every sinner who heartily trusts In Him finds true freedom. *Genuine faith in Christ is the way to freedom from sin's guilt and bondage, and communion with God the Father.* The Israelites' Exodus prefigures these precious spiritual truths.

Indeed, armed with the believing Israelites' understanding of the Triune God, His ways, and His promises, we come to realize the following—God designed the entire history of the people of Israel (not just the Exodus) in such a way as to reveal spiritual truths about Himself and the Christian life through actual, historical events. Of course, this realization isn't anything new.

That's how the apostle Paul used Israel's exodus and wilderness wanderings. Concerning these events, he writes, *"Now these things happened to them as an example, but they were written down for **our** instruction, on whom the end of the ages has come"* (1 Cor. 10:11, emphasis mine). Paul states that these episodes in Israel's history were written down for the instruction of the people who receive his epistles, on whom, he says, the end of the ages (the end times) has come. Therefore, the same is true for us today, as the end times have already begun with the crucifixion and resurrection of the LORD Jesus (cf. Rom. 15:4, where Paul says that all the OT Scriptures were written for *our* instruction and encouragement).

So Israel's entire history should be studied as a representation of the story of *redemption,* with the LORD Jesus giving meaning to everything. We should never forget Jesus' words to the Pharisees. They searched the Scriptures because they thought that in them they would have eternal life, and the LORD told them that it is the OT Scriptures that bear witness about Him as the source of life; yet they refused to come to Him so that they may have life (John 5:39-46). *The Scriptures are an enormous placard, a gigantic billboard sign, which aims to point to Jesus.* A sign is not meant to point to itself. A sign will not have achieved its purpose if the thirsty traveler who approaches it in the middle of the desert stands there, examining every detail of the sign for hours. The sign will have achieved its purpose when the thirsty traveler turns to where the sign points and goes there to find water.

Let us then study Israel's journey after their exodus from Egypt's slavery as such a *billboard sign*. The LORD did not immediately bring the Israelites to the land of Canaan, to the land He had promised to give them. They had to pass through the wilderness first. Those who were covered with the blood of the lamb did not remain in Egypt:

(a) The very next day of Passover, they came out of the land of slavery.
(b) At the same time, the road to the promised land passed through the wilderness.

This is exactly what happens in the life of every sinner when Christ meets him and covers him with His blood:

(a) From this moment onward, the redeemed person does not stay where he was, namely, in the bondage of sin

Jesus saves by His own sacrifice, by His merit *alone*. To His work no one could ever add anything at all. For example, even until the last moment of his life, the apostle Paul deserved eternal hell. And the only reason he is now in heaven is that Christ covered him with His blood. At the same time, the one who has been covered by the blood of Christ, who has tasted forgiveness and freedom from the guilt of sin, is also delivered from the power, the slavery of sin. This is what the precious blood of Jesus achieves. Such a person no longer wants to live in the land of slavery. *They leave from there as their life changes. They do this not to be saved but because they have already been saved, and now they begin to live the new, eternal life that Christ gave them.* The Christian knows that she is not perfect, that she daily needs the grace of Christ. She also knows that the Father accepts her now and forevermore only because of Christ. And based on this priceless Good News, the Christian progresses out of "Egypt," the land of spiritual bondage, and she progresses toward heaven.

(b) At the same time, the Christian is now progressing through the wilderness

Like the ancient Israelites, Christians today live in this world as exiles and pilgrims (1 Pet. 2:11). They yearn for their heavenly homeland and progress toward it through the wilderness. It is worth emphasizing again that Jesus did not promise a life without problems here on earth. Instead, He said, *"I have said these things to you, that in me you may have peace.* **In the world you will have tribulation. But take heart; I have overcome the world"** (John 16:33, emphasis mine).

Therefore, in this wilderness, what we need more than anything else is Him. The only way to advance in this world's wilderness is by having our eyes fixed upon the LORD Jesus. This is what all OT believers invite us to since the life of every OT believer points to Jesus. These people lived by faith in the Christ who was to come, and that is how they reached the finish line. They longed for the heavenly country like Abraham did (Heb. 11:9-10, 13-16).

Often, the OT believers that are mentioned in the eleventh chapter of the epistle to Hebrews are named *"the heroes of the faith."* I am sure they would not accept this title if they could hear it. I imagine them saying, "No, we weren't the heroes. Jesus is the Hero; we owe it all to Him. Do not look to us; look to Him." And that is not just an assumption on my part. The Bible tells us that what is asked of us is not to look to these people but to be encouraged to look to the One they also looked to. Let me repeat that the chapter divisions are a much later addition; they are not part of the Bible. So when we examine the connection between the 11th and 12th chapters of Hebrews, we discover a particularly import-ant truth—that our primary aim should not be to take moral lessons from these people's lives but that *we should be encouraged by them to turn our eyes to the object of their faith, the LORD Jesus.* Hebrews 12:1 begins with the word *"therefore"*. Thus, what follows in the next couple of verses is the conclusion the author of Hebrews draws from the OT believers' expressions of faith he included in chapter 11:

*"**Therefore,** since we are surrounded by so great a cloud of witnesses, let us **also** lay aside every weight, and sin which clings so closely, and **let us run with endurance the race that is set before us, looking to Jesus,** the founder and perfecter of our faith, who for the joy that was set before him endured the cross, despising the shame, and is seated at the right hand of the throne of God."* (Heb. 12:1-2, emphasis mine)

The picture here is that a long-distance race lies before us, which we are to run with endurance toward the finish line. To complete the race, we must lay aside every weight and sin which clings so closely. The cloud of the witnesses of the faith has already completed this race. They surround us; they stand by the track's side. And what they have to say to us is this, "We finished the race because we were believingly and continuously looking to Jesus. Do the same; keep your eyes fixed on Christ."

The following thoughts may assist us in understanding why focusing on OT believers as moral examples is not helpful to our faith. If someone tells us, "You have to believe more," will that help us? If someone tells us, "Here's someone who has a strong faith; imitate him," will then our faith grow stronger? For example, a joke is heard, and everyone starts laughing; then, someone enters the room after the joke has already been told. Can this person sincerely imitate them? If he sees them laughing, does that help him laugh too? Or suppose a theatrical play ends, and the audience begins to applaud enthusiastically; then, someone enters the theater at that time, having missed the play. Seeing others applaud, will this help him heartily applaud as well?

No. We need to hear the joke in order to respond accordingly. We need to see the play for ourselves so that we, too, can erupt in applause (and mean it). In precisely the same way, we need to see with the eyes of our souls Jesus and His overwhelming love for us revealed at Calvary. Then, as a spontaneous response, we will be trusting Him more and more.

That is why *"… faith comes from hearing, and hearing through the word of Christ"* (Rom. 10:17). Because every small piece of Scripture's mosaic shows Christ, the object of the Christian faith. By rightly understanding each piece, our faith grows stronger. The lives of the OT believing Israelites are also such pieces; they also point to the LORD. If we, like them, keep our eyes fixed on Jesus, we will progress and safely reach the finish line where Jesus awaits us with open arms.

* * *

After the events on Mount Sinai, Moses returns to the Israelites, holding in his hands the plates with the ten commandments, which God gave him for the second time. Before embarking on their journey through the wilderness, they must first construct the tent of the tabernacle, also known as the tent of meeting. God gave the construction plans (the "pattern") to Moses at the top of Mount Sinai. The peculiarity of this construction lies in the fact that it is designed to serve as a copy and shadow of the heavenly things and to reflect heavenly realities (Exod. 25:9, 40; Heb. 8:5).

The tabernacle

Indeed, *the tabernacle functions as a three-dimensional presentation of the gospel.* It is structured in such a way as to reveal the coming Messiah. In this construction, Moses originally, and then the high priest of the people, will meet with the LORD, the coming Messiah (it is characteristic that John writes of the eternal Word: *"And the Word became flesh, and dwelt [ancient Greek: tabernacled] among us ... "*—John 1:14).

We will focus on just one *detail* of this tent, which *displays the amazing depth of the greatest story.* The tabernacle (and later the temple of Solomon) was divided into two separate rooms. The first was called "the Holy Place." The second room was called "the Holy of Holies." In it was placed the ark of the Covenant, on which the LORD appeared.

The two rooms were separated by the "veil," a linen curtain. And on this curtain were embroidered *cherubim* (angelic creatures—Exod. 26:31). Through this veil and into the Holy of Holies only the high priest was allowed to pass, once a year only, and only after he had made the sacrifice of atonement for the sins of the people (as described in Leviticus chapter 16).

The symbolism of this structure is especially important. The *veil* symbolized the wall separating the holy God from sinful men. No sinner can approach God without offering a sacrifice first. And this wall was erected the moment the first people turned their backs on the LORD. Then (as we saw in the second chapter), Adam and Eve were expelled from the Garden of Eden; they were removed from the immediate presence of the LORD. They could no longer return, as the entrance to the garden was now guarded by the *cherubim* and the flaming, rotating *sword* (Gen. 3:24). It was precisely this reality that was symbolized by the cherubim that had been embroidered on the veil. For anyone to pass through this curtain, there must be a sacrifice. The flaming sword of God's wrath must fall on someone.

For the veil of separation to be removed and for sinful man to be able to return once again to the presence of God, someone had to pay the cost. And the only one who could do such a thing was the LORD Jesus. Indeed, the incarnate LORD, just a few hours before His crucifixion, foretold to His disciples that the *sword* of God's justice would fall on Him, as was prophesied by Zechariah (cf. Matt. 26:31 with Zech. 13:7). Remarkably, *the moment the LORD died on the cross,* taking upon Himself the righteous wrath of God, *the curtain of the Jerusalem temple was torn in two,* from top to bottom (Matt. 27:50-51). In this symbolic way, God proclaims that the death of Christ achieved the tearing down of the wall that separated God from men. And now, through faith in Christ's blood, we have boldness to enter into the true, heavenly Holy of Holies where Jesus, our great High Priest, is seated (Heb. 10:19-23).

The true High Priest

All this was symbolically revealed by the arrangement of the tabernacle and the service of the High Priest. Just as the Jewish High Priest entered the Holy of Holies with the blood of sacrifice to intercede for the people and ask for the forgiveness of their sins, so the true High Priest, the LORD Jesus, passed through the veil after His bodily resurrection and ascension into heaven. And, being seated on the heavenly throne, He now intercedes for His people, on the basis of His own perfect and unrepeatable sacrifice (Heb. chs. 8 to 10). Now Christ bears on His heart the names of His own and presents them before God the Father. This was symbolized by the breastpiece of the Jewish High Priest, which was worn over his heart. This piece of cloth was covered with twelve precious stones. On each of these stones one of the names of the twelve sons of Jacob was engraved, so that all the tribes of Israel would be presented before the LORD by the High Priest (Exod. 28:15-21, 29-30).

And, of course, *now we can approach God in the name of Christ directly, without the need for other priests or mediators.* For, with the coming of Christ and the completion of His work, the Jewish priestly order was abolished, along with their animal sacrifices. The purpose of this order was to point toward the true High Priest who was to come and His sacrifice. So, when He became incarnate and performed the perfect sacrifice (Jesus, the great High Priest, presented Himself as a sacrifice on the cross, the real altar), this order no longer had a reason for being. The Leviticus priesthood was replaced not by another human order of priests but by the priesthood of Jesus, who is and remains forever our eternal High Priest (Heb. chs. 5 & 7).

* * *

Such details as the tabernacle's and priesthood's typological meaning permeate the Bible and bring into focus the astonishing harmony of the greatest story. The more one comprehends the mind-blowing unity of the Bible, the more one is filled with awe for the Divine Author, who guides both the events and also those who record them. The sixty-six books that comprise the Bible have at least forty human writers who lived from about 1500 BC to about 100 AD. The more one realizes that so many different people collectively wrote such an incredible story of unimaginable depth, which at its center has the perfect Hero, the more one concludes that it takes enormous credulity for the Bible to be considered a mere human construct.

The true Manna from heaven

After the construction of the tabernacle, the Israelites are ready to continue on their path, through the wilderness, to the land of Canaan. Many events mark this journey. The LORD's daily, wonderful provision for His people stands out among them. Every day (except for the Sabbath day), miraculously, the so-called *"manna"* from heaven fell upon the camp of the Israelites. It looked like bread and had a sweet taste. In this way, the Israelites perceived their dependence on the LORD, and day by day, they witnessed His faithfulness. For forty years, throughout their journey, the LORD took care of these people.

With this manna, the LORD saved the people from starvation. Even more important is the reality that manna symbolizes. The Israelites ate from the manna that fell from heaven. At some point, however, they, too, died. *The true manna, the bread from heaven,* the one that if one eats of will never die, *is the LORD Jesus.* The manna points to Him. He said so Himself:

> *"Jesus said to them, **'I am the bread of life; whoever comes to me shall not hunger, and whoever believes in me shall never thirst**. … I am the bread of life. Your fathers ate the manna in the wilderness, and they died. This is the bread that comes down from heaven, so that one may eat of it and not die. I am the living bread that came down from heaven. If anyone eats of this bread, he will live forever. And the*

bread that I will give for the life of the world is my flesh.'" (John 6:35, 48-51, emphasis mine)

Just as God supplied manna in the wilderness to save the Israelites from starvation, so He provided Jesus to save our souls. The LORD is the bread of life. He was torn to pieces on the cross to feed us. He is the bread of life because He has the authority to give true life and because, like bread, He has the power to sustain it. We receive this bread through faith only. As Jesus said, *"Truly, truly, I say to you, **whoever believes has eternal life"*** (John 6:47, emphasis mine). I genuinely believe in Jesus when I receive Him as The One who can satisfy my spiritual hunger and quench my soul's thirst forever. It is essential to nourish our soul daily with Him, the bread of life. *This is exactly why we have the Scriptures; to meet with Jesus, the food of our soul, as we study them with faith.* Let us not despise Him, then, by forsaking Him, the fountain of living waters, and by trying to quench our thirst in broken cisterns that can hold no water. Let us not do as the Israelites did (Jer. 2:13).

The unbelief of the Israelites is an example to be avoided

The Israelites saw incredible miracles. They saw the ten plagues. They saw the Red Sea part in two to pass through its waters. They met the LORD on Mount Sinai. The LORD accompanied them daily. They ate manna every day. And yet, in their overwhelming majority, all this generation of Israelites disbelieved. They constantly turned against Moses and the LORD. They went as far as to say they were better off in Egypt, the land of slavery. And, worst of all, when, after a short period of time, they reached the borders of the land the LORD had promised to give them, the following incident occurred—the Israelites, at the command of the LORD, sent twelve spies into the land of Canaan. They explored the country for forty days. When they returned, ten of them reported that the land was indeed rich and fertile but that its inhabitants were powerful and that it was impossible to defeat them. How great was their unbelief. The other two spies, including Moses' successor, Joshua, told the Israelites there was no reason to fear since the LORD was with them. The people, however, listened to the ten spies, causing them to defect from the LORD (Num. chs. 13 &14). They utterly despised the LORD, so their punishment was to wander in the wilderness for forty years, as many as the days the spies explored the land, until that generation died. Such are the terrible results of unbelief. Forty years later, only the next generation of Israelites will enter the promised land, along with the two spies who trusted the Almighty LORD.

Let us not make the same mistake. Let us not find ourselves outside the land of promise, the new heaven and the new earth (this is what the land of Canaan symbolizes). They heard the gospel, yet it did not benefit them at all, for they did not accept the word they heard with faith. Let us learn from their bad example. As Hebrews 4:1-3a says, *"Therefore, while the promise of entering his rest still stands, let us fear lest any of you should seem to have failed to reach it. For **good news came to us just as to them, but the message they heard did not benefit them, because they were not united by faith with those who listened.** For we who have believed enter that rest ... "* (emphasis mine).

* * *

After forty years in the wilderness, the next generation is on the edge of Canaan. Joshua has succeeded Moses in leadership. He is the one the LORD will use to lead the people of Israel to conquer the promised land. We find these events and the continuation of the narration in the next section of the OT, the books of the Prophets.

The Savior in the Prophets[17]

The conquest of Canaan

The time has come for the words which the LORD had spoken to Abraham to come true: *"Then the LORD said to Abram, 'Know for certain that your offspring will be sojourners in a land that is not theirs and will be servants there, and they will be afflicted for four hundred years. But I will bring judgment on the nation that they serve, and afterward they shall come out with great possessions. As for you, you shall go to your fathers in peace; you shall be buried in a good old age. And they shall come back here in the fourth generation, for the iniquity of the Amorites is not yet complete'"* (Gen. 15:13-16).

These words were spoken when Abraham was still in *the land of Canaan.* About four hundred years later, after the slavery of Egypt has ended, the Israelites (that is, the descendants of Abraham) are ready to return to this land. Indeed, as the LORD had said (Gen. 15:16), the iniquity of the Amorites and the other inhabitants of the land was piling up throughout this time. For centuries, the LORD was patient with those people's sinfulness. How great is divine patience! But their sin was constantly increasing. They were idolaters; they had even gone as far as to sacrifice their children to their false gods. So now the time for judgment has come. The LORD will fight along and through His people to expel these peoples from the land of Canaan. He will use the Israelites to judge the pagan nations justly.

Indeed, during the ensuing years, the Israelites conquer the land of Canaan. The LORD judges these sinful nations and thus fulfills the promise He had given Abraham many centuries ago.

This "holy war" is unrepeatable today, for, during the OT times, the LORD worked through the physical nation of Israel. Today, as the Incarnate LORD declared to Pontius Pilate, *"My kingdom is not of this world"* (John 18:36). His kingdom is and will remain a spiritual kingdom without national borders until His second coming. It is a kingdom consisting of a great multitude that no one could number, from every nation, from all tribes, peoples, and languages, consisting of all those who heartily trust the King.

This unrepeatable holy war issues an intense, urgent warning to us today. For the judgment of these peoples is an exceedingly small fore-shadowing of the judgment that will erupt at the end of this world, at the second coming of the LORD. The LORD continues to be patient with us today. However, one day, as with the Amorites, His patience will end. Thus, our greatest need is *to be reconciled to Him while there is still time.* As the apostle Paul wrote in 2 Corinthians 6:2b (emphasis mine): *"Behold, **now** is the favorable time; behold, **now** is the day of salvation."*

The conquered land of Canaan was the LORD's gift to the people of Israel. A gift they did not deserve (Deut. 9:4-7). He gave them this gift because He loved and chose them. He loved them because He loved them (Deut. 7:6-11), not because they were better than the other nations. And what is asked now of the Israelites is to trust and love the LORD with all their heart and, because they love Him, to keep His good and wise commandments. If they obey, blessings will come to the land of Canaan. If not, if they break the covenant that the LORD Jesus has made with them (Judges 2:1-3), they will suffer the consequences.

The period of the Judges

While Joshua was alive, things were going well. But when he and his generation died, the Israelites abandoned the LORD, the God of their ancestors, who had taken them out of Egypt. They worshiped other gods, those worshiped by the peoples around them, and they followed the abominable pagan customs of the surrounding peoples. As a result, the LORD handed them over to invaders who plundered them. *And here begins a cycle that will continue for the next four hundred years.* Every time the Israelites would abandon the LORD and hence find themselves in a difficult position, they would repent. Then, *the LORD would send them a Judge as their leader,* who would deliver them from the invaders.

For example, in Judges chapter 6, we see the Angel of the LORD, whom the divinely inspired text calls the "LORD," the sent YHWH, speaking face to face with Gideon and sending him to deliver Israel from the Midianites. Furthermore, in chapter 13, the Angel YHWH reveals to Samson's parents, even before Samson is born, that the child they will give birth to will be the next Judge, who will deliver the Israelites from the yoke of the Philistines. In fact, when they ask the Angel of the LORD, "what is your name?", He replies by saying, "My name is *wonderful.*" This *wonderful* God, whom Samson's parents saw with their own eyes (Judges 13:22), was awaited by the believing Israelites to become incarnate (Isa. 9:6) and save them from their sins. They waited for Emmanuel (that is, "God with us"—Isa. 7:14).

As long as the Judge was alive, things were going well. But after he would die, the Israelites would again fall into unbelief and idolatry. And the cycle continued, with the Israelite society sinking into corruption, exploitation of the poor, and lawlessness.

And yet, the Israelites had been given every privilege. The LORD had taken them under His protection and provided them with wise laws and a rich land. If any people had the opportunity to prosper and build a just and flourishing society, it was the Israelites. *Their failure, which was due to their hard-heartedness, reveals the corruption of fallen humanity.*

Likewise, the failure of the Israelites proves how futile it is to hope in human beings, whoever they may be. Indeed, the Judges themselves were not perfect either, far from it. The Bible does not hesitate to record the weaknesses and sins of the individuals whom the LORD makes use of to fulfill His purposes.

Societies in the modern world are not all that different either. Every time people turn away from the true God, as is the case with millions of our fellow citizens today—even though many of them declare themselves religious—judgment is unleashed. A judgment that manifests itself at every level. The only solution is to return to the LORD Jesus, for He is the only hope of the nations. He alone is the rock of ages.

Throughout this challenging period, the believing remnant continues to hope for the Divine Messiah, the true and perfect Judge, who was to come *from the tribe of Judah,* as Jacob, Judah's father, had prophesied (Gen. 49:1, 10). This time, however, has not arrived yet.

The period of the Kings

Four hundred years elapse. The Israelites continue to despise the LORD. They turn to the last Judge, Samuel, and ask him to appoint them a king to rule them "as all nations have" (1 Sam. 8:5). It is not enough for them that the LORD is their King. They want to become like all other nations. Samuel is a pious man. From an early age, his mother had dedicated him to the LORD. The LORD Jesus, the Word of the LORD, met Samuel when he was still a child; He manifested Himself to him and ordained him as His prophet (1 Sam. 3). So, when Samuel hears the request of the Israelites, he does not like it at all, and tries to dissuade them. But they insist. And then the LORD tells Samuel to do what they asked him to do.

God initially appoints Saul as the first king of the people. Saul begins his reign the right way, obeying the LORD. Soon, however, he starts to follow his own path. He does not carry out the commandments of the LORD and, as a result, He rejects him. Samuel announces to Saul that the LORD will take the kingdom from him to give it to someone better than he. *The next king will be young David, the son of Jesse, from the tribe of Judah.* He is still a teenager, the last child of his family, and a shepherd by profession. We are located around 1000 BC.

David, unlike Saul, is a man "after God's own heart." He loves the LORD. He has a genuine, personal relationship with Him and sincerely follows Him. The Psalms he writes, which are included in the OT canon, reveal the deep knowledge of the true Triune God that David has and the way he relates to Him in every circumstance of his life. David will rule Israel for forty years, and during the time of his reign the geographical boundaries of the kingdom will expand more than ever before. In fact, David is chosen by God as the ancestor of the promised Messiah. The LORD promises David that his throne will remain steadfast forever (2 Sam. 7:16) so, from now on, the descendant that the believing Israelites are waiting for is sought in David's lineage. The course of David's life is similar to the LORD Jesus' course of life during His earthly ministry. However, even David is not perfect. Far from it. David goes as far as to commit adultery and murder, for which he repents and receives the LORD's forgiveness. Not even the best king of Israel is sufficient. *Believing Israelites will have to wait for about a thousand more years until the true and perfect King, the LORD Jesus, the descendant of David in the flesh, comes to earth.* As the angel Gabriel had said to the virgin Mary, shortly before she became pregnant and gave birth to Jesus:

> *"And the angel said to her, 'Do not be afraid, Mary, for you have found favor with God. And behold, you will conceive in your womb and bear a son, and you shall call his name Jesus. He will be great and will be called the Son of the Most High. And* **the Lord God will give to him the throne of his father David,** *and he will reign over the house of Jacob forever,* **and of his kingdom there will be no end.**'" (Luke 1:30-33, emphasis mine)

David will be succeeded by his son Solomon. His own kingdom will be peaceful, and in his time, the temple of Jerusalem will be built. Very quickly, however, things will take the wrong turn.

Immediately after Solomon's death, the kingdom of Israel will be broken up. In the south, the southern kingdom will consist of the tribes of Judah and Benjamin, while the remaining ten tribes of Israel will gather in the northern kingdom. From now on, the kings of both the northern and southern kingdoms, as a rule, will lead the people to idolatry, with only a few bright exceptions, which, however, are not enough to make a difference.

Prophets sent to the two kingdoms

During this troubled period, the LORD sends prophets to *the two kingdoms.* Their mission is to call the Israelites to return to the LORD. They warn them of their disobedience's consequences and also give amazing promises about the coming Divine Messiah and His kingdom. The prophets speak openly and courageously, and that is why they face the hostility of a large part of the people. People have always loved the darkness rather than the light (John 3:19-20). Despite all resistance, the prophets will continue their mission. This is because the message they preach is not theirs but the LORD's.

Among other things, the prophets *warn* the people of Israel that, *if they continue in disobedience,* the northern and southern kingdoms will be overthrown by hostile nations, the nation will be captured, and *the Israelites will be driven into exile.* And indeed, that is what happens. The Assyrians conquered the northern kingdom in 722 BC and forced its inhabitants to disperse to the various territories of the Assyrian empire. The southern kingdom, the kingdom of Judah, will endure a little longer, but in the sixth century BC, it will also be captured by the superpower of the time, the Babylonians. The Babylonians destroyed the temple that Solomon had built and led much of the people into *exile.*

Exile and return

Exile is bound to cause despair among the Israelites. They wonder what God is doing and whether He has forgotten His promises. As David's throne no longer exists, his lineage is in immediate danger. And this is so crucial, for the LORD had promised that the Divine Messiah was to be born from this lineage. But the LORD always remains faithful to His word. There is no way He will make a promise that will not come true. *The exile would end seventy years later* (just as Jeremiah, who acted before and during the fall of the kingdom of Judah, had prophesied—Jer. 29:10) *in a truly miraculous way.* In 538

BC, the Persians subjugated the Babylonians and conquered their land. Then, the Persian king Cyrus ordered in writing the *return* of the Jews from exile to Jerusalem and the reconstruction of the temple that the Babylonians had destroyed. We read the narration:

> *"And [the Babylonians] burned the house of God and broke down the wall of Jerusalem and burned all its palaces with fire and destroyed all its precious vessels. [The king of the Chaldeans] took into exile in Babylon those who had escaped from the sword, and they became servants to him and to his sons until the establishment of the kingdom of Persia,* **to fulfill the word of the LORD by the mouth of Jeremiah,** *until the land had enjoyed its Sabbaths. All the days that it lay desolate it kept Sabbath,* **to fulfill seventy years.** *Now in the first year of Cyrus king of Persia,* **that the word of the LORD by the mouth of Jeremiah might be fulfilled, the LORD stirred up the spirit of Cyrus king of Persia,** *so that he made a proclamation throughout all his kingdom and also put it in writing: 'Thus says Cyrus king of Persia, 'The LORD, the God of heaven, has given me all the kingdoms of the earth, and* **he has charged me to build him a house at Jerusalem,** *which is in Judah. Whoever is among you of all his people, may the LORD his God be with him. Let him go up.'""* (2 Chr. 36:19-23, emphasis mine)

Cyrus justifies his decision in a surprising way. This heathen king declares that *the LORD commanded him* to build a temple in Jerusalem. The way the LORD's commandment reaches the Persian king Cyrus is even more astonishing. According to the Jewish historian Josephus,[18] who lived in the first century AD, *Cyrus read the prophecy of Isaiah* (see Isa. 44:28), as the Israelites had carried the Scriptures with them into exile. At that point in the book of the prophet Isaiah, *the LORD addresses Cyrus by name* and orders him to rebuild the temple. The significance of this fact is understood when we realize the period the prophet Isaiah wrote his book. Isaiah acts from 736 to 700 BC approximately. That is, *more than 150 years earlier than the time of king Cyrus.* And yet, he mentions him by name—another proof of God's inconceivable omnipotence. Truly, *the LORD is the Lord of history.* This is what king Cyrus understands and willingly obeys, thus ending the seventy year exile of the Jews.

Indeed, *the prophet Isaiah* lived long before the fall of the kingdom of Judah. So, it is remarkable that he prophesied the Babylonian captivity as a punishment because of the disobedience of the nation and the subsequent exile and return from it. What is even more remarkable is that he prophesied far beyond the events of the Babylonian exile and restoration; *he prophesied of the coming Divine Messiah and Redeemer.*

Isaiah's prophecy: Jesus, the Messianic King who becomes the suffering Servant

In the beginning of his book, Isaiah describes his breathtaking encounter with the LORD in the temple (Isa. 6). Isaiah, humanly speaking, had every reason to be afraid. The king of Judah had died at that time (6:1), and the neighboring hostile nations were lurking. And as if this weren't enough, as he enters Jerusalem's temple Isaiah sees with his own eyes the King, the LORD of hosts, sitting upon a throne, high and lifted up. Above Him stood angelic seraphim who, covering their faces, cried out, *"Holy, holy, holy is the LORD of hosts; the whole earth is full of his glory!"* The majesty of the LORD's glory crushes him. And while he exclaims, *"Woe is me! For I am lost; for I am a man of unclean lips ... for my eyes have seen the King, the LORD of hosts,"* one of the seraphim touches the prophet's lips with a burning coal that he had taken with tongs from the altar. In this symbolic way, he assures him that "his guilt is taken away, and his sin atoned for." This gesture's symbolism lies in the fact that the altar points to the ultimate place of sacrifice, Calvary. Isaiah had every reason to be afraid, yet the great King meets him in his fearful state. The LORD presents Himself to Isaiah in his hour of need precisely in the way that the prophet needs to see Him, as the Almighty King who has the authority to forgive sins. And He sends him to preach the truth; the truth about who the LORD is, and how He will save His people from their sins.

Isaiah firstly revealed the LORD sitting "upon a throne, *high and lifted up*" (ch. 6). In the second part of his book, in an astoundingly detailed prophecy, he reveals the servant of the LORD, the Divine Messiah, as one who *"shall be high and lifted up, and shall be exalted"* (52:13). He shall be exalted, after having first taken upon Himself the wrath of God, after having been punished on behalf and in the place of His people, after having been crushed for our sins, that we may be healed with His wounds (53:1-8). Who cannot discern in this prophecy the sacrifice of Jesus, His glorious resurrection, and His wonderful intercession for transgressors (53:9-12)?[19] Indeed, the suffering Servant *now* "stands high and lifted up" (same expression in 6:1 and 52:13) as He reigns from the tree. He reigns victoriously as He keeps sprinkling many nations with His life-giving blood (52:15).

Who is the LORD of hosts Isaiah shows in chapter 6? Who is the suffering Servant of the second part of this prophetic book? Of course, He is the LORD Jesus. He is the one Isaiah saw, and he wrote about Him. To dissipate any remaining doubts, the twelfth chapter of the Gospel according to John combines quotations from Isaiah chapters 6 and 53 (see John 12:36-41). John then concludes his argument by saying, *"Isaiah said these things because he saw [Jesus'] glory and spoke of him"* (John 12:41).

Indeed, the great King used His inconceivable authority to become the servant King. *"… [he] came not to be served but **to serve, and to give his life as a ransom for many"*** (Matt. 20:28, emphasis mine). He came to die for and in the place of His rebellious subjects. *He was lifted up* on the cross and, hanging on that tree, He manifested the apex of His glory to those who have eyes to see. He gave His precious blood to deliver His own from the power of darkness and to now reign in their hearts and lives. *Who can compare to this Lord?*

Also, Isaiah records that the Messiah will be born of a virgin and will be called "Emmanuel," a name that means "God with us" (Isa. 7:14).

Furthermore, he prophesies about this Son: *"For to us a child is born, to us a son is given; and the government shall be upon his shoulder, and his name shall be called* **Wonderful Counselor, Mighty God, Everlasting Father, Prince of Peace.** *Of the increase of his government and of peace there will be no end, on the throne of David and over his kingdom, to establish it and to uphold it with justice and with righteousness from this time forth and forevermore.* **The zeal of the LORD of hosts will do this"** (Isa. 9:6-7, emphasis mine).

In this passage, Isaiah states that the name of this child who will be born and have all authority will be "Mighty God" (9:6). He then goes on to say that the LORD of hosts (the first Person of the Trinity) will do this (9:7). Isaiah, thus, knows that the true God is not a unipersonal being and he anticipates the birth of the God-man Messiah.

Not only that, but *Isaiah is given the privilege to record the words of the Most High God to the Messiah* in Isaiah 42:1: *"Behold my servant, whom I uphold, my chosen, in whom my soul delights; I have put my Spirit upon him; he will bring forth justice to the nations"* (cf. with Jesus' baptism: Luke 3:21-22).

As if that weren't enough, Isaiah also *records the words of the Messiah Himself,* the sent LORD. Indeed, in Isaiah 48:12-13 & 16, the LORD Jesus says unto Israel, *"Listen to me, O Jacob, and Israel, whom I called!* **I am he; I am the first, and I am the last.** *My hand laid the foundation of the earth, and my right hand spread out the heavens; when I call to them, they stand forth together... Draw near to me, hear this: from the beginning I have not spoken in secret, from the time it came to be I have been there.'* **And now the Lord GOD has sent me, and his Spirit"** (emphasis mine).

Isn't it amazing? The Creator of Israel, the I AM, the First and the Last, declares that the Lord GOD [the Father] has sent Him [the Christ—that is, the anointed one], together with His Spirit [the Holy Spirit].

Isaiah expresses a deep understanding both of the three Divine Persons and of the nature and mission of Christ, in whom he himself hopes. It is no coincidence that Isaiah has been named "the fifth evangelist.' Indeed, in chapter 61, Isaiah recorded the words of the LORD (there is no break between chapters 60 and 61, the LORD keeps on speaking—see Isa. 60:22 for the speaker's identity). These are the words of Christ Himself, as proven by the fact that centuries later, in a synagogue, the incarnate LORD, the Christ (anointed with the Holy Spirit), stood up to read them. He unrolled the scroll of the prophet Isaiah, found this passage, and declared:

> *"The Spirit of the LORD is upon Me,*
> *Because He has anointed Me*
> *To preach the gospel to the poor;*
> *He has sent Me to heal the brokenhearted,*
> *To proclaim liberty to the captives*
> *And recovery of sight to the blind,*
> *To set at liberty those who are oppressed;*
> *To proclaim the acceptable year of the LORD."*
> (Luke 4:18-19 NKJV, quoted from Isa. 61:1-2a)

Then, after reading these words, Jesus boldly states for all to hear, *"Today this Scripture has been fulfilled in your hearing"* (Luke 4:21).

Dear reader, the LORD Jesus is the promised Messiah. He is the only one with the required power and will "to heal the brokenhearted." Thanks to His death and resurrection, Jesus continues to liberate and heal by His Gospel and Spirit—to this day. Come to Him with simple, humble faith either for the first time or once again to find in Him everything you really need.

The promise of the New Covenant is the solution to humanity's hard-heartedness

After seventy years of exile, the Israelites return to Jerusalem and Judea. Not because they deserve it, but thanks to the mercy of the LORD. Their purpose is to reconstruct the temple and the city of Jerusalem and restore its walls. They will encounter many difficulties in this effort. At some point, however, the temple will be completed.

Their biggest problem, though, is not the state of the Jerusalem temple but their hard-heartedness. At every opportunity and on every occasion, *the vast majority of the people denies the LORD.* They ignore His commandments and turn away from Him. The Jewish community is again immersed in immorality and thus transgresses the covenant that the LORD had made with them on Mount Sinai. The Israelites are no different from other pagan nations. Despite everything that has happened, their hearts have not changed; they remain hard and corrupted. And *for their situation to change, it takes much more than rebuilding the temple.* The One, who is the true Temple, needs to come; that is, the LORD Jesus (John 2:21). *He needs to come so that He may seal the New Covenant with His shed blood.*

Throughout the ages, this Covenant has been the only solution to humankind's hard-heartedness. For even today, everyone who is without Christ is an idolater. Even those who declare themselves to be atheist worship someone or something. Their object of worship may be the approval of others, social status, comfort, relationships, wealth, career, sports, family, health, their own self, or anything else, good or bad, which takes the first place in the life of man. The question for every man is not *whether* he worships but *what* he worships. *Jeremiah and Ezekiel prophesy about this New Covenant,* which we all desperately need.

The *prophet Jeremiah* knows firsthand the hard-heartedness of the Israelites. The LORD has sent him to warn them of the coming exile if they continue in their sins. They remain unrepentant, and Jeremiah experiences with them the disaster that follows. At the same time, he envisions the days when the Messiah will come (the phrase "after those days" refers to the Messianic age—Jer. 31:33). And he prophesies that, *"after those days," the LORD will make a new covenant.* We read about this New Covenant:

> *"Behold, the days are coming, declares the LORD, when I will make* ***a*** > ***new covenant*** *with the house of Israel and the house of Judah,* ***not like*** > ***the covenant*** *that I made with their fathers on the day when I took*

them by the hand to bring them out of the land of Egypt, **my covenant that they broke,** *though I was their husband, declares the LORD. For this is the covenant that I will make with the house of Israel* **after those days,** *declares the LORD:* **I will put my law within them, and I will write it on their hearts. And I will be their God, and they shall be my people.** *And no longer shall each one teach his neighbor and each his brother, saying, 'Know the LORD,' for they shall all know me, from the least of them to the greatest, declares the LORD. For I will forgive their iniquity, and I will remember their sin no more."* (Jer. 31:31-34, emphasis mine)

The first covenant, the covenant made on Mount Sinai where the Israelites received the Law, did not have the power to change the Israelites' hearts. So they transgressed that covenant. And consequently, they were driven into exile. And yet God promises restoration. He promises a New Covenant, which will differ from the first. The enormous difference of the New Covenant is that all who belong to it will know the LORD personally and that the LORD will write the law in their hearts so that they shall obey Him (Jer. 31:33). As a result, the members of the New Covenant will never break this covenant, contrary to what happened in the first (Jer. 31:31). The members of the New Covenant comprise the spiritual Israel; that is, all the believing Jews and Gentiles throughout the centuries. The most fundamental reason that all New Covenant members enjoy and experience these blessings is given in Jeremiah 31:34, as this verse starts with the word *"for."* It is because the LORD has *already* forgiven their iniquity and will never again remember their sins to condemn them that these promises are true.

In order for forgiveness to be given, however, someone had to pay the cost. Someone had to experience the judgment we deserve to be exiled. Someone had to pass through exile and take us with Him to the restoration. And the only one who could ever achieve such a thing is none other than the promised Messiah, the God-man Jesus. He is truly the Mediator of the New Covenant, as He declared the night before His crucifixion, *"this is my blood of the covenant, which is poured out for many for the forgiveness of sins"* (Matt. 26:28, emphasis mine). He was exiled from the Father's presence when nailed to the tree so that we, though we deserve the punishment of eternal hell, might receive the promises of restoration and eternal dwelling in the presence of God, who has now become "our God." Indeed, based solely upon His precious, shed blood and His subsequent resurrection, Jesus freely bestows eternal forgiveness. And also, through His Spirit, He graciously (that is, for free!) gives new, abundant, true, eternal life to every sinner who will trust solely in Him.

The New Covenant-related prophecies are first symbolically fulfilled in the history of the Jews when they return from the Babylonian exile. And then, they *find their complete fulfillment in the work of the incarnate Christ.* Indeed, it was revealed to the Prophets by the Spirit of Christ, who was in them, that they wrote about Jesus (1 Pet. 1:10-12). The NT Scriptures confirm that this is the correct understanding of these prophecies. In the letter to Hebrews (8:6-13; 10:15-25), its author quotes the verses we have already seen from Jeremiah 31 to assure us that Jesus is the mediator of a better covenant and that whoever believes in Him has *already* entered this covenant and has *already* received the forgiveness of sins. And in Galatians, the apostle Paul tells us that all these blessings are bestowed upon both Jews and Gentiles *the moment someone becomes united with the LORD Jesus through faith alone* (Gal. 3:8-9, 14, 27-29). In fact, in the same chapter, Paul tells us that by hearing the Good News about the crucified Savior with faith, we receive the Holy Spirit (3:1-5).

How a person becomes a Christian

Here we stand before a precious truth; a person is not born a Christian, nor is she a Christian because her ID card says so, nor because she was once baptized or repeated the words of a prayer, nor because she goes to a church. *A person becomes a Christian when she hears the Good News with genuine faith and receives Jesus* as her *Savior* and the *Lord* of her life, saving her from the wrath of God. At that moment, Christ meets her, places her inside the New Covenant, forgives her, and gives her new, eternal life.

Afterward, what is asked of every true Christian is to continue living the new life the LORD gave them in precisely the same way it began—by faith. That is, by believing in Christ and His promises. We receive the Holy Spirit when we turn with faith to Christ. In the same way, the Holy Spirit continues to act more and more in our lives as we increasingly understand the Savior's greatness and the gospel's unimaginable depth. The gospel is not the ABC of the Christian life; it is the A to Z. As the gospel takes root in our hearts, the Spirit leads us to trust exclusively in Christ and not in ourselves and in what we do or don't do.

Indeed, *it is the gift of the Holy Spirit that makes the New Covenant entirely effective against the hard-heartedness of men.* The risen and exalted Jesus has received from the Father the promise of the Holy Spirit, whom He is now pouring out upon all His people (Acts 2:33). It is the Holy Spirit, the third Person of the Holy Trinity, who opens the spiritual eyes of blind men and gives them a new heart so that they can see the beauty of Christ and love Him. It is the Divine Comforter who leads Christians to a life of hearty trust and obedience.

The blessings of the New Covenant

The prophets Ezekiel and Jeremiah describe these *blessings* of the New Covenant. Ezekiel acted during the period of exile. In chapter 36, *Ezekiel* records the words of the LORD in the first person:

> *"I will sprinkle clean water on you, and you shall be clean from all your uncleannesses, and from all your idols I will cleanse you. **And I will give you a new heart,** and a new spirit I will put within you. And I will remove the heart of stone from your flesh and give you a heart of flesh. **And I will put my Spirit within you, and cause you to walk***

in my statutes and be careful to obey my rules" (Ezek. 36:25-27, emphasis mine).

This passage is similar to Jeremiah 31:31-34. They both express precious truths intended to encourage all true Christians, assure them of God's love for them, and lead them to trust entirely in the great Savior and nowhere else. Christian, do not trust in yourself in the least. Don't trust in your own faith either. Instead, trust in the true God to keep you faithful to the end. He promises to do so! Indeed, *the LORD Himself declares that the final preservation of believers is part of the many New Covenant blessings.* God, through *Jeremiah,* in chapter 32, states that the eternal covenant He has made with believers has a *dual purpose:*

- To put His fear in our hearts *so that we will not turn from Him*
- To always do good to us with all His heart.

*"… they shall be my people, and I will be their God. **I will give them one heart and one way, that they may fear me forever,** for their own good and the good of their children after them. **I will make with them an everlasting covenant,** that I will not turn away from doing good to them. **And I will put the fear of me in their hearts, that they may not turn from me*** (LXX: apostatize, depart, fall away). ***I will rejoice in doing them good,*** *and I will plant them in this land in faithfulness,* **with all my heart and all my soul"** (Jer. 32:38-41, emphasis mine).

These promises are so priceless that it is worth quoting them in full. Sometimes we may think that God barely tolerates us. And yet, He confirms to every Christian that it is His joy to do always and only good to His people, in every circumstance (Rom. 8:28-29). Indeed, He promises to do good to us with all His heart and infinite power. No one would dare to believe such a thing if the LORD Himself had not promised it to us—and God's promises are irrevocable, for they are bought and sealed with the precious blood of the LORD. How good

Jesus is. How great the Father's love for His children is. Therefore, if God is for us, who can be against us (Rom. 8:31)?

The New Covenant's Mediator

We owe *all* New Covenant blessings to the New Covenant's magnificent Mediator, the promised Messiah. The Prophets never mention the blessings of the New Covenant *without also presenting the beauty and majesty of the Messiah.*

Jeremiah, in chapter 23, conveys the words of the Father about the coming Messiah. Here, Jesus is named as "Branch," the descendant of David (as already prophesied by Isaiah—cf. Isa. 11:1). In this passage, the Father says that He will raise this Branch to reign as king, and that in His days Israel will be saved. Additionally, He says that one of the Branch's wonderful titles will be, *"the LORD* (Yahweh) *is our righteousness"* (Jer. 23:5-6, emphasis mine). At this point, we should no longer be surprised by the deep understanding of the Trinity we find in the writings of the Prophets.

Ezekiel, too, records the words of the Lord GOD, the Most High God. These words are conveyed to Ezekiel by the Word, since the text begins as follows: *"And the word of the LORD came to me, saying ..."* (Ezek. 34:1 NKJV), which is an accurate translation of the Hebrew. In chapter 34, the prophet records the Father's words. Here, the LORD speaks against the shepherds of Israel, for they, instead of caring for His sheep, actually live at their expense by devouring the LORD's people (Ezek. 34:1-10). And the LORD says that He will come to search for and shepherd His sheep (Ezek. 34:11-22). Immediately afterward, He reveals that the One who will shepherd His people is "His servant David." Therefore, it is the Messiah, the descendant of David according to the flesh, who will be the ruler of the people, on behalf of the LORD (Ezek. 34:23-24).

The LORD Jesus, the Branch of David, *is the good Shepherd of the Sheep.* He is the One who came to sacrifice His life for the sake of the sheep. He is the One who came to seek and to save the lost (Luke 19:10). The lost sheep couldn't do anything to help themselves. Thus, Jesus Christ did it all for them, and He now proclaims to His sheep, *"I give them eternal life, and they will never perish, and no one will snatch them out of my hand. My Father, who has given them to me, is greater than all, and no one is able to snatch them out of the Father's hand"* (John 10:28-29, emphasis mine).

The Good Shepherd came to seek and to save the lost so that they shall be lost no more and shall never perish. The Good Shepherd *guarantees* the salvation of His sheep. And He wants us to be certain that nothing and no one will ever separate us from His love (Rom. 8:35-39) so that we may trust Him, no matter what our circumstances may be, and joyfully follow Him.

But how can the LORD make such promises? How can He declare that *He will forgive the iniquity of His people and will no longer remember their sin?* (Something we saw in Jeremiah's prophecy about the New Covenant—Jer. 31:34.) In other words, how is it possible for Him to promise that He will never condemn His own for their sins?

Of course, the Omniscient LORD does not suffer from amnesia, and because He loves His children so much, He will not hesitate to discipline them for their good when necessary (Heb. 12:1-11). At the same time, however, the promise is clear, and the question remains—how can it be true that those included in the New Covenant *will never be condemned for their sins?* What has the LORD Jesus done so that He can declare, *"Truly, truly, I say to you, whoever hears my word and believes him who sent me **has eternal life. He does not come into judgment, but has passed from death to life"*** (John 5:24, emphasis mine).

The answer to this question leads, and will lead, the LORD's people to *eternal* worship. The Bible's answer is that the LORD did *everything* on behalf of and in the place of His sheep so that He now gives them such astonishing promises. And when we say "everything," we do mean "everything."

On the one hand, as we have seen so clearly thus far, the LORD, with the precious blood of His sacrifice on the Cross, paid for and erased once and for all the guilt for *all* the sins of *all* His people (Col. 2:13-14)—*sins of the present, past, and future.* If this were not the case, what would be the alternative? Should we pay ourselves for the rest of our sins? If I believed in luck, I would say, "Good luck." If the LORD had not done everything, there would have been *no* Good News. Praise His name, for His perfect sacrifice is enough and, therefore, there is no need to add anything to it. And, *based upon this sacrifice, the LORD gives complete, eternal forgiveness to all believing sinners, the moment they turn to Him with genuine trust.*

And on the other hand, the LORD does not stop with forgiveness. If He stayed there, He would merely bring us back to square one, which would mean that we would now have to try to obey so that in the end, if we had obeyed enough, we would be accepted. Again, I would say, "Good luck," for the Law of God requires perfection (Deut. 27:26; Gal. 3:10-14) from our first to our last breath. And, certainly, perfection not only in words and deeds but also in thoughts, feelings, desires, and motives. Therefore, man's effort is never enough, however strenuous it may be. For nothing less than absolute perfection will ever be accepted in the presence of the Holy, Perfect God. This perfection, *this perfect righteousness,* which all of us so desperately need and yet are so incapable of even approaching, *is bestowed by the LORD Jesus completely free of charge on all those who trust in Him.* In fact, Jesus gives us Himself to *be* our righteousness. Therefore, as we saw in Jeremiah, one of the titles of the Messiah is, "The LORD, our righteousness."

To become "our righteousness," the LORD became incarnate in the fullness of time. He was born under the Law to become accountable to the Law (Gal. 4:4-5). All this to obey the Law, in order to fulfill a perfect righteousness on behalf of His people. Therefore, Jesus, by obeying in the place of all who trust in Him, succeeded in redeeming them from the curse of the Law. For with this righteousness, with this perfect obedience, Christ "clothes" those who are united with Him by faith.

The Good News: Justification by faith alone in Christ

Here is the GOOD NEWS; *here is what it means to say that Jesus did "everything" to save His people*—the Law requires punishment for every transgression. Christ received on the cross the punishment that sinners deserve. The Law also requires perfect obedience to its commandments. The LORD obeyed perfectly. And now, resurrected, having fulfilled all the requirements of the Divine Law, He bestows His righteousness on all sinners who will trust in Him alone.

For someone to truly trust in Christ, he first needs to understand two things. First, his absolute inability to do anything to save himself, and second, that the LORD is the perfectly sufficient Savior and, thus, worthy of his absolute trust. Only then will sinners cease to trust anywhere else and heartily turn to the Savior. And then, they will have boldness to stand before God the Father. For the Father of Christ will have also become their Father by *adoption.* All people are (rebellious) creatures of God the Father, but *only those who receive His Son by faith become His children,* that is, those who are "*in Christ*" (John 1:12-13; Gal. 3:26-4:7).

God the Father treated His Son on the cross as we deserve to be treated. And as He clothes us with the righteousness of Jesus, He now treats us as Jesus Christ Himself deserves to be treated. All this becomes ours by faith alone in Jesus Christ alone (Gal. 2:16; 3:8-9); that is, *as we believingly receive Jesus to be our righteousness.* And from this moment, and for all eternity, the Father sees us united with Christ, covered with Jesus' own worth. *Here is the Good News*—justification (i.e., perfect acceptance by God the Father forever) by grace alone, through faith alone in Jesus Christ alone.

In the heavenly court

The precious truth of justification through faith alone because of Christ alone (that is, salvation by the work of Christ and **not** *by the works of man*) is found in every part of the Bible. We saw it in the Pentateuch

(Gen. 15:6), and we will see it in the next section of this chapter in the Psalms (Ps. 32) and in the NT epistles. Prior to turning, however, to the Psalms, we will examine an *astonishing image from the heavenly court, an image that illustrates justification by faith alone in the most illuminating and dramatic way.*

This image is conveyed by the prophet Zechariah, who acted toward the end of the sixth century BC, after the return from the Babylonian exile. In Zechariah chapter 1, we meet a well-known Person, the Angel of the LORD. That is, the LORD Jesus, before His incarnation (the Word without flesh—"Logos asarkos"). In Zechariah 1:12 the sent LORD intercedes for Jerusalem, as He addresses Himself to the LORD of hosts, to God the Father.

It is worth noting that verses like this one, which record the Son's conversations with the Father, do not merely contain some hints about the Trinity, which we who now have the NT writings can discern. All these OT Scriptures require to be read as the revelation of a multi-personal God. Since the true God is Triune, the same must always be true of His self-revelation also.

Back to verse 1:12, the Angel of the LORD asks the LORD to show mercy toward Jerusalem after the Jews had suffered for seventy years in exile. And the LORD of hosts answers with comforting words (1:12-17). Zechariah, however, finds the greatest consolation in the words of the Messiah, the Angel of the LORD, which he records in the second chapter. There, the sent LORD says that, from the wonderful works He will do, the Israelites will know that the LORD of hosts sent Him to them (2:9-11) and that He who will be sent will come to dwell with His people. He is the Messiah, the humble, righteous king who saves (cf. Zech. 9:9). And immediately after that, in chapter 3, we find the aforementioned scene that takes place in the *heavenly court.* With this scene, *the LORD visually explains* to the prophet Zechariah, and by extension to all the readers of this prophetic book, *how He justifies and saves sinners.*

In chapter 3, we see the Israelite high priest of that period. His appearance reveals the wretched state of the priesthood and the people he represents. In 3:1, this high priest stands before the Angel of the LORD. His filthy garments symbolize his sinfulness (3:3). He stands before the LORD to plead for mercy, as he has nothing good of himself to present. And this is confirmed by the fact that to the right of the high priest stands the devil to resist him and accuse him. His accusations are true. He doesn't have to lie. The high priest is guilty. And yet, at this moment, the LORD Angel says to the devil: *"And the LORD said to Satan, 'The LORD rebuke you, O Satan! The LORD who has chosen Jerusalem rebuke you! Is not this a brand plucked from the fire?'"* (Zech. 3:2).

The LORD has chosen Jerusalem and the high priest, and He will save him as someone plucks a brand from the fire. He will save him by taking away the high priest's iniquity and by clothing him with His glorious righteousness. In this way, *the Judge of the universe will proclaim in the heavenly court that this sinful man is **righteous**,* as indicated by the following verse: *"And the [A]ngel said to those who were standing before him, 'Remove the filthy garments from him.' And to him he said, **'Behold, I have taken your iniquity away from you, and I will clothe you with pure vestments'"*** (Zech. 3:4, emphasis mine).

Here is how the LORD Jesus saves: He takes away the iniquity of all who turn to Him to be saved, and at the same time, He covers them with "pure vestments," that is, with His perfect righteousness. And also, He assures them by His truth and Spirit that they have been forgiven, just as He did with this high priest. And then man has peace with God (Rom. 5:1), and the more he knows and thinks of the truth expressed by the words of the apostle Paul, *"Who shall bring any charge against God's elect? **It is God who justifies**"* (Rom. 8:33, emphasis mine), the more he is filled with supernatural joy.

All this is given entirely freely to sinners, for Jesus paid it all for them on the cross (Rom. 8:34). Indeed, the LORD Himself, hundreds of years before the Romans invented the horrific penalty of crucifixion, had revealed that He would be *pierced.* Zechariah recorded the prophetic words of the LORD: *"And I will pour out on the house of David and the inhabitants of Jerusalem a spirit of grace and pleas for mercy, so that,* **when they look on me, on him whom they have pierced,** *they shall mourn for him, as one mourns for an only child, and weep bitterly over him, as one weeps over a firstborn"* (Zech. 12:10, emphasis mine).

When a sinful man understands what happened on the cross, he is crushed, for he realizes that *because of his own sins,* Christ was nailed to the tree and "pierced," as the prophecy said (John 19:34-37). And he mourns for the pain he inflicted on the Lord of the universe. And also, he is filled with unspeakable joy as he realizes that *Christ did not only die because of him but for his sake also,* so that now an opened fountain exists (Zech. 13:1), filled with the blood of God (cf. Acts 20:28). For only the blood of the cross can cleanse from all sin and uncleanness. And only the righteousness of Christ can constitute man righteous in the heavenly court.

Everything we have said about justification is summarily expressed in question 70 of the Westminster Larger Catechism[20] (1648 AD):

Question 70. What is justification?
Answer: Justification is an act of God's free grace unto sinners, in which he pardoneth all their sins, accepteth and accounteth their persons righteous in his sight; not for anything wrought in them, or done by them, but only for the perfect obedience and full satisfaction of Christ, by God imputed to them, and received by faith alone.

* * *

The Israelites who returned to Jerusalem after the Babylonian captivity completed the temple's construction during the ensuing years. They remain, however, under enemy occupation. They have not been able to regain their independence. The majority of the people are indifferent to or hostile toward the LORD. At the same time, a faithful remnant longs for the coming of the Messiah. In this context, toward the end of the fifth century BC, one of the last OT books was written (as far as the date of authorship is concerned)—*the book of the prophet Malachi.*

Malachi's message is convicting. He calls the Israelites to repentance so that the coming of the Messiah will not bring judgment to them but salvation. At the same time, *he records the words of the LORD to the Israelites: "Behold, I send my messenger, and he will prepare the way before me. And the Lord whom you seek will suddenly come to his temple; and the messenger of the covenant in whom you delight, behold, he is coming, says the LORD of hosts"* (Mal. 3:1).

With these words, the LORD Jesus declares that, after His angel/ messenger (John the Baptist) has come to prepare the way before Him, *the LORD Himself will come to His temple,* the Angel of the Covenant, for whom the believing Israelites were waiting. After Malachi's prophetic book, about four hundred years will pass. During this time, no more prophets will be sent to Israel. But *the faithful remnant, from generation to generation, will await the fulfillment of the messianic promises.* Indeed, shortly before the beginning of the incarnate LORD's earthly ministry, John the Baptist, the LORD's messenger, appears, just as Malachi had prophesied four centuries ago (Mal. 4:5-6; cf. Matt. 11:14, 17:11; Mark 9:11; Luke 1:17). John, like Malachi before him, will also call the people to repentance in order to prepare the way of the God-man.

Before we turn our focus to the NT era, it is worth studying what the OT's last section, the section of the Psalms, reveals about the ultimate Hero of the greatest story.

The Savior in the Psalms[21]

A large part of the book called Psalms was written by King David, the man after God's own heart. So the Psalms began to be written in about 1000 BC. Perhaps one would have expected that such old texts would be obsolete by now, that they would have nothing important to teach us. And yet, in the Psalms, the Christian faith is expressed in the form

106

of poetry. And the Psalms are of such unique literary value that, with their profound truths, they touch not only our minds but also our hearts.

Like the rest of the Bible, the truths we find in the Psalms focus on the Person and work of the LORD Jesus. *All 150 Psalms are Messianic,* for both David (2 Sam. 23:2; Acts 2:30) and their other authors were prophets (1 Chr. 25:1-5). Therefore, what would have been strange would be if the Psalms had not had as their central theme the great Savior, the ultimate Hero of the greatest story.

Christ is the central theme of the Psalms since with these 150 poems:

(a) We sing *to* Jesus
(b) We sing *of* Jesus
(c) We sing *with* Jesus.[22]

(a) We sing *to* Jesus in the Psalms

We have already seen that both the Pentateuch and the books of the Prophets have a rich Trinitarian, Christocentric theology. The same is true of the Psalms. So when we sing the Psalms with proper understanding, *we sing to Jesus.* When the authors of the Psalms address God as our Rock, our Shepherd, our Judge, our Shield, our Creator, our Refuge, our Fortress, our Defender, our Healer and Supplier of all our needs, and our Redeemer, *they glorify the LORD Jesus.*

Indeed, the authors of the Psalms were well aware of who the God they worship truly is. In the second Psalm, we see the LORD (God the Father) and Christ, the anointed of the LORD, His Son. The Psalmist even records the Father's promise to the Son: *"Ask of me, and I will make the nations your heritage, and the ends of the earth your possession"* (Ps. 2:8).

Similarly, David in the *one hundred and tenth Psalm* records the words of the Father to the LORD Jesus: *"The LORD says to my Lord: 'Sit at my right hand, until I make your enemies your footstool'"* (Ps. 110:1).

Also, *Psalm 45* speaks of the King and His bride. What is remarkably interesting is that the author, addressing the King, the anointed (Christ) of God (45:7), says: ***"Your throne, O God, is forever and ever. The scepter of your kingdom is a scepter of uprightness;*** *you have loved righteousness and hated wickedness.* ***Therefore God, your God, has anointed you with the oil of gladness ..."*** (Pss. 45:6-7, emphasis mine). Once again, it is clear that the author recognizes two distinct Divine Persons. In fact, these verses are used in the first chapter of Hebrews (1:8-9) to prove that Jesus is God the Son. Let us further dive into this Psalm.

Psalm 45: Jesus, the heavenly Bridegroom

Some think that Psalm 45 concerns Solomon, the son of David; yet the King who is praised is called "God" and the Psalmist explicitly states that the King's throne is eternal. Charles Spurgeon's comment on this Psalm is illuminating:

> "Some here see Solomon and Pharaoh's daughter only—they are short-sighted; others see both Solomon and Christ—they are cross-eyed; well-focused spiritual eyes see here Jesus only, or if Solomon be present at all, it must be like those hazy shadows of passers-by which cross the face of the camera and therefore are dimly traceable upon a photographic landscape. "The King," the God Whose throne is forever and ever, is no mere mortal, and His everlasting dominion is not bounded by Lebanon and Egypt's river. This is no wedding song of earthly nuptials, but an epithalamium for the heavenly Bridegroom and His elect spouse."[23]

Seen under this light, the Psalmist's words toward the Bride express the King Jesus' desire: *"Hear, O daughter, and consider, and incline your ear: forget your people and your father's house, and* ***the king will desire your beauty.*** *Since he is your lord, bow to him"* (Pss. 45:10-11, emphasis mine). The LORD Jesus continues to address these words to every member of His Bride, the Church (that is, to all believers in Christ). How astonishing the LORD is. He sees His Bride as beautiful and desires her beauty, even though the church is still full of wrinkles and blemishes. How wonderful it is for the Lord of the universe to continuously desire His people with such intense fervor!

Just from these examples, it becomes clear that the authors of the Psalms understand very well the meaning of their writings (as do all OT authors). They do not speak better than they know. They speak as well as they know.

Based on their understanding, the Psalmists and, by extension, *all OT believers sing to Jesus with assured hope and trust.* This accords with all the Scriptures, given that the Bible never speaks of hope as an uncertain possibility that may or may not happen (e.g., 1 Pet. 1:3-4; 1 John 3:3). The hope God bestows on His people is certain and unwavering, for it depends only on His unchanging character and His irrevocable promises. Therefore, we do not find in the Psalms expressions that would fit into a religion of works. The Psalmists approach their Holy LORD and God in awe and fear, and also with genuine joy and intimacy. They are confident in their relationship with God. This is because they do not rely on their own works. They do not ground their relationship with the true God on what they themselves do or don't do; that is, on their obedience. Instead, they depend solely on the goodness and mercy of the LORD and Savior toward them.

For example, we referred earlier to the second Psalm, where we met the Christ of the LORD, the Son. This Psalm closes with the following words to all: *"Kiss the Son, lest he be angry, and you perish in the way, for his wrath is quickly kindled. Blessed are all who take refuge in him"* (Ps. 2:12). Those who insist on their unbelief to the Son, which is the greatest sin and the source of all iniquity, will perish. On the contrary, blessed in the eyes of God (regardless of any difficult circumstances they may face) are those who "take refuge in the Son." That is, all those who put their confident trust in Christ—in Christ and nowhere and no one else.

Those who trust in Christ are led to love Him. For they know experientially, and not only theoretically, Christ's love for them. To the extent that Christ's church knows Him and understands Christ's passionate love for her, to the same extent, the church (and each believer) will respond with love, adoration, gratitude, worship, trust, and obedience.

Song of Songs: a hymn to Christ's love for His Church

As we have already seen, *Christ's love* for His church is described in Psalm 45. It is also portrayed in the *Song of Songs,* another book of the Psalms OT section. To this book, the church turned, for millennia, in order to taste the love of Christ. The contemporary church is equally in need of the Song of Songs. For there we see the relationship of the Messiah with His Bride expressed in such a poetic way that His love can melt even the hardest heart. In fact, at one point, the words of the woman's response to this love are recorded: *"I am my beloved's, and his desire is for me"* (Song of Sol. 7:10).

Genuine Christians know they belong to Jesus and have begun to understand that the LORD loves them with such intensity that human words are too poor to describe. This is equally true both for genuine Christians living after Christ's incarnation and for those who lived during the OT era.

This should come as no surprise to us, as the Psalms's authors and all the OT-believing Israelites experienced the same Christian faith we have. Their faith and love for Christ made the authors of the Psalms sing to Jesus with certain, assured hope. They knew that, even though they were sinful people, at the same time, they were blessed by God, for they had the Son as their Savior. And so, they sang to Him with joy, confident of where they stood before God. David expressed the precious truth of gracious, free acceptance by God in Psalms 51 and 32.

Psalm 51: true repentance

Psalm 51 is known as the Psalm of repentance. It is the Psalm that David wrote when the prophet Nathan rebuked him for his guilt. David was indeed guilty. He had committed adultery with Bathsheba, the wife of Uriah, one of David's military officers. This occurred while Uriah was away from home, fighting in the war. David, being commander-in-chief, was supposed to be on the battlefield. He neglected his duties and ended up in sin. And as if adultery weren't enough, when he learned that he had left this woman pregnant, in order to cover his tracks, he gave orders to leave Uriah alone on the front line of the battle so that the enemy's soldiers would kill him. David was, therefore, guilty of adultery and murder. And it was necessary, about a year later, for the prophet to show him his sin so that finally David would come to his senses, understand that the punishment for his crimes should be death, and repent. Then Nathan assures him that the LORD overlooked his sin: *"David said to Nathan, 'I have sinned against the LORD.' And Nathan said to David, **'The LORD also has put away your sin;** you shall not die'"* (2 Sam. 12:13, emphasis mine).

The consequences of David's sin will henceforth follow him and his family, as the LORD declared (2 Sam. 12:1-18). These consequences will be severe and will last for many generations. Because David had utterly scorned the LORD, the child who was born would die. And yet, the LORD forgave him, overlooked David's sin, and took away his guilt. Indeed, forgiveness was given immediately the moment David confessed his sin to the LORD. Nothing else was asked from him. *How differently the LORD deals with His own than any religious person would expect.*

It was at this moment in his life that David wrote Psalm 51. It was probably the prayer he addressed to God as soon as he admitted his guilt. He had heard the comforting words of the prophet, *"The LORD also has put away your sin; you shall not die."* However, the burden of guilt continued to press on his heart, his conscience. So he pleads with the LORD to cleanse him of his iniquity (51:2) and purge him with hyssop (51:7). Hyssop reminds us of the night of the Exodus, when with branches of hyssop the Israelites sprinkled the doors of their houses with the blood of the lamb. David symbolically pleads with the LORD to sprinkle his conscience with the blood of Christ. He does not try to justify himself; he throws himself entirely upon the mercy of

God (51:1). He confesses he sinned against his own Savior (51:4). The LORD had given him all things, and David, by his actions, despised Him. But David knows that the LORD can relieve him of the burden of guilt. That is why he runs to Him whom he had hitherto despised. He pleads with the LORD to change him; to create in him a pure heart (51:10), and to give him once again the joy of his salvation (51:12). He does not ask the LORD to save him but to restore to him the joy of salvation. Finally, he pleads with the LORD to enable him to teach His ways and for sinners to return to God (51:13-15).

David's repentance is genuine, as shown by the fact that he himself chooses to make this Psalm public, with which *he exemplifies what true repentance is* and demonstrates how to return to the LORD either for the first time or once again. *"Repentance"* literally means *a change of mind.* Its biblical sense is a change in how man sees himself, his life, other people, and above all, a change in his attitude toward God and sin. It is a profound, internal change, touching the core of man's existence. Now man recognizes that he is deserving of God's wrath, sees his need for Christ, realizes that Jesus is enough, and runs to Him in faith, as David did. David knew that God would not accept any sacrifice he could offer (51:16). But he also knew that the LORD would never despise a broken and contrite heart (51:17).

David was crushed for his sin when he finally admitted that he had sinned against the LORD, against the One who had shown him such kindness. And the LORD continued to show David His grace by forgiving him the moment David confessed his sin. It is clear that repentance is not a series of works, whatever they may be, that man must do so that God may finally forgive him. The changed life is the result of repentance—deeds are the *fruit* of repentance (Matt. 3:8; Acts 26:20). *Repentance itself, however, is the inner change that only God can work in a man's soul* (2 Tim. 2:25-26).

This is why the Psalms are filled with so much joy, and the Psalmists are full of trust in the LORD. They are people who live in the age of the Law, but they do not relate to God on the basis of what they themselves do or do not do. What was true of David then continues to apply today. David did not go to a priest to confess, he did not ask for the intercession of any man (dead or alive), he did not do "penance" as false religion requires, he did not trust in any sacrament, and he did not pray anywhere else, except directly and personally to the LORD, his Savior. *Such straight dealing with the LORD was, is, and will always be the only way to salvation.*

Even at the worst moment of his life, David was under the LORD's care. Jesus never ceased to love him, so He did whatever it took for David not to perish. God loves His children so much that even if they go astray, He will intervene so that they do not continue on the path to destruction. David remained a child of God, even during his lapse. In order to bring him to his senses, the LORD took away from him the joy of salvation, the joy of personal fellowship with Him. So, while David was trying to hide and justify his sin, he lived in misery and sorrow during all those months, as the fatherly hand of the LORD was heavy on him, intending to correct him. David himself tells us this in Psalm 32:3-4, as *Psalm 32* should most likely be placed after Psalm 51, chronologically.

Psalm 32: true blessedness

After the LORD convicted David through the words of the prophet Nathan, David uncovered his sins before the LORD, and the burden was removed from his soul: *"I acknowledged my sin to you, and I did not cover my iniquity; I said, 'I will confess my transgressions to the LORD,' and you forgave the iniquity of my sin. Selah"* (Ps. 32:5, emphasis mine).

Through this ordeal, David personally experienced the grace and mercy of the LORD and understood even better what *true blessedness* is. And through the words of David, God reveals to us also who the truly blessed man is: *"**Blessed** is the one whose transgression is forgiven, whose sin is covered. **Blessed** is the man against whom the LORD counts no iniquity, and in whose spirit there is no deceit"* (Ps. 32:1-2).

Blessed are not those who have riches, power, intelligence, beauty, fame, or glory. *Blessed* are those who have peace with God. And the only ones who have peace with God are those whose sins the LORD has covered. Those who, even though they have committed iniquities, the LORD does not count them against them. He does not count them against them because Christ bore their sins in His body on the tree as they were imputed to Him. And at the same time, the merit, the righteousness of Christ, is accounted to everyone who trusts in Him (2 Cor. 5:19-21).

David was covered with the righteousness of Christ, and that was enough to be eternally accepted by God the Father. And all this solely by faith in Christ, which is why David writes, *"... steadfast love surrounds the one who* **trusts** *in the LORD"* (Ps. 32:10b, emphasis mine). In fact, when the apostle Paul wants to affirm that justification is by faith and not by works, he quotes David's words from Psalm 32:1-2, explaining that *"... David also speaks of the blessing of the one to whom* **God counts righteousness apart from works**" (Rom. 4:6, emphasis mine).

Psalm 32: the true Gospel

This is the GOOD NEWS; this is the true GOSPEL. *The true Gospel sets true Christianity apart from false substitutes.* And unfortunately, there are many such. Each heresy distorts the truth about Jesus Christ and/or His work. Everyone who denies that the LORD Jesus is the second Person of the Trinity who became incarnate, very God of very God, is in darkness. Equally lost is everyone who denies that Christ's work is unrepeatable and perfect, that Jesus is perfectly sufficient, and that man does not need, and indeed cannot, add anything to what Christ has already achieved with His death on the cross and His bodily resurrection from the dead; that sinners receive the LORD Jesus by faith alone. The apostle Paul emphatically declares that *man is righteous apart from works* by quoting David's words from Psalm 32:1-2. What is striking is that David wrote those words many years after his conversion, when he had already performed a number of good deeds.

What of good works, then? The one who trusts in Christ and has received the forgiveness of his sins, precisely because he knows that his sins have been forgiven, has the power to overcome them. That is why he lives the new life that Christ has given him—that is why he now lives differently. *His good works are the fruit and, thus, the proof of salvation. But whoever preaches that man must do good works to be saved and/or to maintain his salvation distorts the true Gospel,* and is under the anathema (that is, the condemnation), which the apostle Paul placed upon all false teachers who preach "another gospel" (Gal. 1:6-9).

The Gospel of salvation by grace alone, through faith alone, in Jesus Christ alone is what we find in the Psalms. Such gracious salvation was a present reality then because the precious blood of Christ was applied by the Holy Spirit to the souls of men thousands of years before the crucifixion, as it is applied today thousands of years after Jesus' death. And, because all this has been revealed to them, *the Psalmists joyfully praise the LORD, their Redeemer,* the great Savior for great sinners, as David was. And they invite all the "righteous," that is, all who trust and love Christ, to *"Be glad in the LORD, and rejoice ... "* (Ps. 32:11).

(b) We sing *of* Jesus in the Psalms

The Psalms speak of the Messiah, the Christ. So, when we sing the Psalms, *we sing about Jesus and His work.* The Christ of the LORD is presented as King in Psalm 2, and Psalm 110:1 focuses on the Messianic King, as was already seen. The "Lord" who is superior to His father David is the Divine Messiah (Mark 12:35-37; cf. Heb. 1:13, which quotes Ps. 110:1).

The Psalms describe in detail the life and work of the incarnate Jesus:

- *Psalm 8* praises Christ as the Man to whom God has given authority (Heb. 2:6-9; 1 Cor. 15:27).
- *Psalms 2 and 110* speak of Jesus' messianic kingdom (Acts 4:25-28; Heb. 1:5, 13; Matt. 22:44; Acts 2:34-35).

- *Psalm 118* prophesies Christ's triumphant entry in Jerusalem and the Father's election of Jesus as the cornerstone (Matt. 21:9, 42; 1 Pet. 2:7-8).
- *Psalm 41* refers to Judas' betrayal of Christ (John 13:18).
- *Psalm 22* describes the scene of the crucifixion as Jesus experienced it on the cross (cf. 22:1 with Matt. 27:46), but also the subsequent heavenly glory, as the Lamb who was slain is now the worship Leader of His church (cf. 22:22 with Heb. 2:12).
- *Psalm 16* prophesies His resurrection (Acts 2:23-36, 13:35-39).
- *Psalm 24* praises the "King of Glory," who, having ascended to the LORD's mountain, is ready to come in the everlasting doors. This is an incredible description of the LORD Jesus' heavenly ascension and enthronement.
- *Psalm 96* (among others) declares that all tribes, languages, peoples, and nations of the earth must come and will come to the LORD with praise and thanksgiving.
- *Psalm 98* glorifies the resurrected King as He comes to judge the world.

Every Christian who reads the Bible in the same way that the LORD Jesus and the apostles read it finds in the Psalms Christ's life, death, resurrection, ascension, present government, and His second coming. So, *when Christians praise the LORD by singing the Psalms with the correct understanding, they sing about the LORD Jesus Christ and His work, about the Savior who had to suffer and then rise from the dead.*

(c) We sing *with* Jesus in the Psalms

In the Psalms, we not only sing to Jesus and sing of Jesus, but *we also sing with Jesus.* This is true because *the Psalms describe Jesus' experiences during His earthly ministry.* The Psalms were the hymnbook of Jesus with which He was perfectly familiar, as can be seen by how often He referred to them, even during His last moment on the cross. And the Psalms can describe and express the thoughts and feelings of Jesus because God directed the lives and thoughts of the Psalmists in such a way that their words prophetically anticipate the events of Jesus' life.

The Psalms, then, open a window that allows us to discern the inner workings of the soul of the incarnate LORD. The four Gospels focus primarily on the outward, public life of Christ, but the Psalms reveal to us the secrets of His thoughts and feelings. How poorer we would be in terms of knowing the LORD if we had not had the Psalms in our hands!

The LORD used all the Psalms to express His worship of God the Father. *There are, however, Psalms that literally contain the words of Jesus.* These Psalms do not reference historical events in their authors' lives. On the contrary, the Psalmists, since they were prophets, recorded the words of the incarnate LORD. *Examples of such Psalms are Psalms 22 and 16.*

Psalm 22: the horror and greatness of the Cross

Psalm 22 has appropriately been called "the Psalm of the Cross."[24] In it, we find another perspective of what happened during the crucifixion. The Gospels describe what was going on around the cross. Psalm 22, however, allows us to see things through someone else's eyes; *through the eyes of Him who hung on the wood of the cross.* The first words of this Psalm are precisely the words that the LORD cried out while darkness had covered the earth, *"My God, my God, why have you forsaken me?"* (Ps. 22:1a, quoted in Matt. 27:46). In the words of this Psalm, therefore, we discern the excruciating pain, anguish, and sorrow that Jesus experiences. He, the Son of the Father's love, looks to heaven and, for the first time in His life, does not see the smile of the Father but His fiery wrath. The burning waves of God's righteous wrath erupt one after another with all their inconceivable force against Christ, to the last one. At that hour, God *forsakes* His Son, who stands condemned in the place of sinners. The Father *forsakes* His Son so that He will never *forsake* those sinners who find refuge in the shadow of the Cross (Heb. 13:5). The Cross is the only safe place on earth because there the wrath of God has already been unleashed.

Psalm 22 carries the same prophetic power as Isaiah's 53rd chapter. Within its verses, we observe the LORD Jesus trusting God amidst unfathomable darkness and agony. Those gathered around the cross mock Him (22:7; cf. with Matt. 27:39). They say, *"He trusts in the LORD; let him deliver him; let him rescue him, for he delights in him"* (22:8; cf. with Matt. 27:43). The anguish of Jesus is such that He says, *"But I am a worm and not a man, scorned by mankind and despised by the people. ... I am poured out like water, and all my bones are out of joint; my heart is like wax; it is melted within my breast; my strength is dried up like a potsherd, and my tongue sticks to my jaws; you lay me in the dust of death"* (22:6, 14-15). How much pain do these words reveal? How incomprehensible the magnitude of the humiliation of the Lord of the universe is. And how inscrutable the love He shows toward His rebellious creatures is. He sees the soldiers dividing His garments among them and casting lots for His tunic (22:18, cf. with Matt. 27:35; John 19:23-24). And yet, He remains faithful to His mission. He could have called a legion of angels. At any time, He could have come down from the cross. Even so, He chose to drink the bitter cup to the end. He chose to stay nailed to that blood-stained cross until He paid the debt and completed the work of redemption. And only then did He cry out, *"It is finished"* (John 19:30) and committed His spirit to His Father (Luke 23:46).

And yet, Psalm 22 does not end at the crucifixion. It goes on to describe the glories that would follow. The Psalmist records the words of the risen Christ, the great Mediator: *"I will tell of your name to my brothers; in the midst of the congregation I will praise you"* (22:22). The author of Hebrews assures us that these are the words of Jesus (Heb. 2:12). *The risen Jesus stands in the midst of His Church and leads her to praise God the Father.* Jesus is the true worship leader. He sings with us! Perhaps this explains why Christians love to gather and sing *together* to their God even if they do not have any musical training—a remarkable phenomenon that is not easily encountered among other social groups. In response to His amazing work, Christians sing to the LORD, and their joy reaches its apex. Not only that, but God Himself is among them, singing with them (Zeph. 3:17). So, the time will come when, thanks to the work of Christ, people from every nation and from all ends of the earth will gather around Jesus to worship Him and the Father forever, as this beautiful Psalm describes in closing (22:26-31).

It is clear that the words of Psalm 22 do not concern the circumstances of David, its author. He may have suffered in his life, but nothing can be compared to what these words describe. The correct understanding of the Psalm is that it refers to the crucifixion of the LORD. Besides, David writes: *"… dogs encompass me; a company of evildoers encircles me;* ***they have pierced my hands and feet"*** (22:16, emphasis mine). David never experienced anything like this. Being a prophet, however, he spoke of the horrors of the cross centuries before the Romans conceived this brutal method of torture and execution. William Binnie's comment on this Psalm is worth mentioning:

> "The only adequate and natural interpretation of the psalm [22] is that which sees in it a lyrical prediction of the Sufferings of Messiah and the Glory that was to follow. No Sufferer but One could, without presumption, have expected his griefs to result in the conversion of nations to God."[25]

Psalm 16: the triumph of the Resurrection

The same applies to Psalm 16. In fact, the title given to it in the Syriac and Arabic translations was "concerning the election of the church, and the resurrection of Christ."[26] We know that the words of this Psalm belong to Jesus, for they could not suit anyone else. For example, verse 10 could not be applied to David, the author of the Psalm: *"… my flesh also dwells secure. For you will not abandon my soul to Sheol, or let your holy one see corruption"* (16:9b-10). This is precisely the apostle Peter's argument on the day of Pentecost, fifty days after Christ's resurrection from the dead. When on that day the Holy Spirit came with power upon the apostles and they began to speak foreign languages, Peter addressed the gathered crowd and quoted these verses from Psalm 16 (cf. Acts 2:26-27, 31) to prove that the Bible had prophesied Christ's resurrection:

> *"For **David says concerning him** [Jesus], "'I saw the Lord always before me, for he is at my right hand that I may not be shaken; therefore my heart was glad, and my tongue rejoiced; my flesh also will dwell in hope. For you will not abandon my soul to Hades, or let your Holy One see corruption. You have made known to me the paths of life; you will make me full of gladness with your presence.'" 'Brothers, I may say to you with confidence about the patriarch David that he both died and was buried, and his tomb is with us to this day. **Being therefore a prophet,** and knowing that God had sworn with an oath to him that he would set one of his descendants on his throne, **he foresaw and spoke about the resurrection of the Christ, that he was not abandoned to Hades, nor did his flesh see corruption.** This Jesus God raised up, and of that we all are witnesses.'"* (Acts 2:25-32, emphasis mine)

Peter emphasizes to the Jews, some of whom were personally responsible for Jesus' crucifixion, that all this was done according to the Scriptures since David did not speak of himself in Psalm 16. After he died, he was buried, and his flesh saw corruption. David wrote about Christ, and indeed Christ did not stay in the tomb, as death could not hold the One who is the Author of life. *Since Jesus rose from the dead on the third day, His body did not see corruption.* The Jews who heard this and knew the Scriptures did not object to Peter's words. Instead, the truth that Peter so courageously preached to them convicted them and led them to repentance. On that day, three thousand people returned to the risen LORD (Acts 2:41). All this took place inside the city where Jesus had been crucified, only a few days after His death.

Indeed, *David, being a prophet, recorded the words of Christ.* Jesus conquered the fear of death by trusting in God's promise that He would not leave His body in the tomb. Thus, His soul was filled with joy during His earthly ministry in the thought that what awaited Him after death was His return to glory and the inconceivable joy of God's immediate presence (Ps. 16:11).

This is where the LORD Jesus now is. Where there are "pleasures forevermore," for by His resurrection, He defeated death. And all this for the sake of "His saints" (Ps. 16:3). That is, for the sake of all true Christians, since *all genuine Christians are called saints* (set apart for God) because of their faith-union with Christ. *This is how the term "saint" is used throughout the Bible.* Any other understanding stems from mistaken human traditions. In fact, this verse (16:3) reveals the heart of Christ toward His Bride, His church. There, the LORD says that all His delight is in the saints, namely, all those who heartily trust in Him. *Christ's love for His Bride is so boundless that it proved to be stronger even than death itself.*

As the Psalms express the full breadth of the LORD's feelings, they simultaneously give the words to Christians to do likewise. Since all genuine Christians are united with Christ, they share common experiences with Him and benefit from His wonderful redemptive work. Thus, having seen Psalm 16 with the understanding that these are the words of Jesus, we can now see these words as the expression of the Christian experience of David and every believer. Such is the identification of the Head with the body that, in the Psalms, we hear the voice of Christ and the Church in the same words. As Augustine (354–430 AD) wrote, *"the voice of Christ and his Church was well-nigh the only voice to be heard in the Psalms."*[27] By believing in Christ (Ps. 16:1, 8), every Christian overcomes the fear of death and can have peace and contentment even in the most challenging situations (16:5-6). And even though the bodies of Christians see corruption when they die, because of Christ and through their union with Him, they will experience the miracle of resurrection from the dead in the second coming of the LORD. And then, the words of the Psalm that apply to Christ (16:10-11) will fully apply to His own as well.

* * *

The Psalms truly help us better understand the spiritual life of the incarnate Jesus, the great Hero. And they give us the privilege of singing hymns from His hymnbook. As His *body*, we sing to Jesus, sing of Jesus, and at the same time *sing with Jesus, our Head*. As pastor Michael Lefebvre put it, "In all the Psalms (and only in the Psalms) we have words of Christ to sing with him … We find Jesus in the Psalms by hearing his voice leading our praise in every line."[28] *Verily, Jesus is our true worship leader.*

It is fascinating to observe that the Author of the greatest story makes sure to reveal sides of the multifaceted majesty of this story's ultimate *Hero* in every section of the Bible, as this story unfolds. Indeed, in the Bible, God makes known not only the historical events of the public life of the central Hero, but even His inner life, namely, His thoughts and emotions. And all this was prophesied and recorded in the Pentateuch, the Prophets, and the Psalms hundreds of years before the incarnation of Jesus. *We will now see the fulfillment of all these OT prophecies and promises concerning the Messiah as we turn our attention to the NT books.*

The Savior in the NT books

The Gospels—the fulfillment of the Messianic prophecies

The last OT book was written in about 400 BC. Since then, and until the incarnation of Jesus, about four hundred years elapse. *During these centuries, God has kept a faithful remnant to Himself.* These people *hold tightly to the OT promises* of the coming Messiah. And they pass them on from generation to generation, until the fullness of time. Then, the LORD Jesus came to become like us *to fulfill all the OT Messianic prophecies and promises* (1 Pet. 1:10-12; 2 Cor. 1:19-20). (For references to members of this believing remnant who were waiting the coming Redeemer of Israel, see Luke 2:25-32, 36-38; John 1:45, 11:27.)

In fact, Emmanuel (i.e., God with us) was born of the Virgin Mary by the Holy Spirit (in fulfillment of Isa. 7:14, cf. with Matt. 1:22-23) in the city of Bethlehem in Judea (in fulfillment of the prophecy of Micah 5:2-4, cf. with Matt. 2:1-6) from the tribe of Judah (in fulfillment of Gen. 49:10) from the lineage of David (in fulfillment of the words of the LORD to David, 2 Sam. 7:16 and the prophecies of Isaiah 9:6-7 and Jeremiah 23:5-6, cf. with Luke 1:30-33, 3:23-38; Matt. 1:1-17) by both of His earthly parents. He was named "Jesus" after divine command (Matt. 1:20-25), a name that signified who He is and what His mission was (since, as we have seen, the name "Jesus" means in Hebrew "the LORD saves").

Throughout *His earthly ministry,* Jesus proclaimed the truth with unprecedented authority (Matt. 7:28-29). And His words were accompanied by incredible signs and wonders, which proved His identity. He gave the blind their sight, the deaf their hearing, speech to the mutes, He cleansed lepers, made the lame to walk, delivered the demon-possessed, evangelized the poor, and raised the dead. Indeed, even death itself fled away from His presence. All this in fulfillment of the prophecies about the Messiah (Isa. 35, 26:19, 61; cf. with Luke 7:11-27). All these signs, and many more, revealed that Jesus *is* the light of the world, the bread of life, the source of living water, the truth, the resurrection, and the life—the promised Messiah.

In fact, Jesus, in His conversation with the Samaritan woman, proclaimed that He is the Messiah (John 4, cf. with Matt. 26:62-66). Some people say that Jesus never claimed to be God. If they had understood that the OT presents the Messiah as the Divine Person who bears the name "The LORD, our righteousness" (Jer. 23:5-6), they would have never made such a claim. Equally extraordinary is the truth that *Jesus is the only person in the whole of human history that people from every corner of the earth accept as the Messiah.*

Moreover, not only did Jesus proclaim with His words and prove by His deeds that He is the Messiah, but *He also repeatedly spoke to His disciples about His impending death and resurrection.* This truth is recorded in all four Gospels. For instance: *"And taking the twelve, [Jesus] said to them, 'See, we are going up to Jerusalem, and **everything that is written about the Son of Man by the prophets will be accomplished.** For he will be delivered over to the Gentiles and will be mocked and shamefully treated and spit upon. And after flogging him, they will kill him, and on the third day he will rise'"* (Luke 18:31-33, emphasis mine).

This is exactly what the Prophets had written, as we have already seen—that Christ will be rejected (Isa. 53), die in the most horrible way (Ps. 22), and then rise from the dead (Ps. 16).

Jesus knew perfectly well what was going to happen to Him as He was going to Jerusalem for the last time, and yet He did not back down. Because that is why He had come; He had come *to die*. And He *had* to die, for there was no other way to save sinners. And since He knew what awaited Him, we see Him the night before His arrest experiencing unthinkable agony in the garden of Gethsemane (Matt. 26:36-46; Luke 22:39-46). He tells His disciples that *"[His] soul is very sorrowful, even to death"* (Matt. 26:38a). Such was His anguish that His sweat became like drops of blood and fell on the ground. He pleaded with His Father to remove from Him, if it be possible, the cup that was before Him. The LORD was not in such agony merely about the physical sufferings of the crucifixion, even though they were indescribably horrific. Death by crucifixion is so horribly and inhumanely torturous that, if we were present in such a scene, we would most likely faint in the face of such an abominable spectacle. Still, many Christians faced calmly such a terrible death with the courage the LORD bestowed upon them. It was something else that caused the Lord of the universe to agonize to such an extent. It was the content of the cup, which, in that garden, He perceived so vividly and clearly. *It was the cup of God's wrath* (that is what the "cup" symbolizes throughout the Bible—Jer. 25:15; Isa. 51:17; Ps. 11:6; Rev. 14:10-11, 16:19). *This is what awaited Christ on the cross, and that is why He was so sorrowful.* That cup was filled with the wrath that our sins pile up against us daily. Sins of all kinds. Murders, adulteries, thefts, immoralities, lies, idle words, and offensive thoughts. All this deserves God's punishment, which would erupt on Christ, a few hours later, *at the hill of Golgotha.*

Judas Iscariot, one of the twelve disciples of Christ, betrayed Him that night, as Scripture had foretold (Ps. 41:9, cf. with John 13:18). What followed was an unjust trial, a parody of a trial, where they were seeking testimony against Jesus to put Him to death, but they found none. In the end, after being questioned by the high priest, Jesus confesses that He is the Christ, the Son of God. The priests knew that with these words Jesus was declaring He is the God-man, the prophesied Messiah. The Christ stood before them, but they were too blind to see, therefore they accused Him of blasphemy for telling the truth about Himself (Mark 14:53-65).

And so, the only Innocent and Righteous is condemned to death by crucifixion. Throughout this process the LORD remained silent before His accusers, like a lamb that is led to the slaughter (Isa. 53:7). They spat at Him, mocked Him, beat Him, whipped Him. And all this was done just as the Servant LORD, speaking through Isaiah 700 years before His incarnation, had prophesied that would happen to Him (Isa. 50:4-7). And after putting on His head a crown of thorns, the Roman soldiers led Him to *Calvary*, where they nailed Him to the cross.

On that cross, Christ, hanging between heaven and earth, standing condemned and stripped of all dignity, took the cup He had seen in the garden of Gethsemane—the *cup* filled with the righteous wrath of God the Father. *And He drank it to the last drop.* There, the Father crushed His Son (Isa. 53:10). This is why God has absolutely no vengeful wrath against His children. This is why *"There is therefore now no condemnation for those who are in Christ Jesus"* (Rom. 8:1). For the LORD suffered for us, for our sins, so that in His wounds we might find healing. Just as Isaiah had prophesied:

> *"Surely he has borne our griefs and carried our sorrows; yet we esteemed him stricken, smitten by God, and afflicted. But he was pierced for our transgressions; he was crushed for our iniquities; upon him was the chastisement that brought us peace, and **with his wounds we are healed.** All we like sheep have gone astray; we have turned—every one—to his own way; and **the LORD has laid on him the iniquity of us all.**"* (Isa. 53:4-6, emphasis mine)

And as Isaiah had also prophesied, the LORD "was numbered with the transgressors" since He was crucified between two criminals (cf. Isa. 53:12 with Luke 22:37; 23:32-33). And yet, He was not buried with the wicked. Instead, after the Roman soldiers confirmed His death, they handed over the body of Christ to one of His disciples, following the command of Pontius Pilate. This disciple was called Joseph of Arimathea. He was a rich man, and so he was able, after taking the body of Christ, to place it in his own new tomb, which he had cut in the rock (cf. Isa. 53:9).

This tomb, which had been sealed with a great stone—this tomb, which Roman soldiers guarded—was found empty on the third day after the crucifixion of Jesus (Matt. 27:57-28:6). This is because *the LORD Jesus was bodily resurrected from the dead* as He himself had prophesied and all the Scriptures had foretold (1 Cor. 15:1-8).

The historical fact of Jesus' bodily resurrection

In the context of so many fulfilled prophecies, of so many divine promises, of such historical events, the *resurrection* of Jesus no longer seems absurd. On the contrary, it is the only *logical* explanation for the events that took place then and those that have been occurring since then. This is the case because the historical facts are indeed specific:

- Jesus was crucified and buried.
- His tomb was found empty.
- His disciples claimed that they saw the risen Jesus repeatedly during a period of forty days, until He ascended to heaven.
- Just a handful of His disciples (the apostle Paul, writing in 55 AD, mentions five hundred eyewitnesses of the resurrected Christ—1 Cor. 15:6), starting from Jerusalem—the city where these events took place—spread throughout the then known world with the message of Jesus' bodily resurrection and the forgiveness that He bestows. And even under persecution (because the exclusivity that Christ demands as the sole Lord provokes this kind of reaction) the Christian faith rapidly spread throughout the Roman Empire.

No other answer can explain these historical events,[29] which forever changed the course of history, *except the bodily resurrection of Jesus from the dead.* And the historical event of Jesus' resurrection is the *cornerstone* of Christianity. If Jesus had not been raised from the dead, then, as the apostle Paul says, Christians would have been *"of all people most to be pitied"* (1 Cor. 15:19).

Acts of the Apostles—the spread of the Gospel

Following the four Gospels, the book titled *The Acts of the Apostles* describes the rapid spread of the Gospel as the risen LORD acts through the Holy Spirit and His disciples so that they may fulfill *the great commission.* That is, to make disciples of Christ from all nations, preaching the Good News to all the world. This is the commission that the risen LORD gave His church and every one of His disciples (Matt. 28:16-20; Mark 16:15; Luke 24:46-48; John 20:21; Acts 1:8). From that time until today, from word of mouth, from place to place, and from generation to generation, the Good News of the resurrected Savior is spread, as the LORD is building His church.

It is worth pointing out that nowhere does the NT use the term "church" to refer to buildings. Instead, it applies it to people, to all believers in Christ. This is because the third Person of the Trinity, the Holy Spirit, indwells every genuine Christian (Rom. 8:9). And so, *Christians,* both individually (1 Cor. 6:19) and collectively (1 Cor. 3:16-17), are *the holy temple of God.*

No one is saved by belonging to some religious denomination. Christ saves each person individually, the moment that person hears the Good News and receives Christ through faith. At that moment, the person is united with Christ, and becomes a member of His body. And so, he becomes a member of His universal church (meaning all of God's born-again children throughout the world). And at the same time, because the universal church of Christ is expressed in local churches (assemblies) of believers where the true Gospel is preached, every genuine Christian has a desire to belong to a true, healthy local church.

A *local church* that is rooted in the Gospel is the best apologetic for the value and truth of the Gospel. This is because those who are united *by faith* with the Christ of the Gospel, who is the living Stone, become themselves "living stones." And so, united with each other, they are built up as a spiritual house, they become a "holy priesthood," and offer spiritual sacrifices that God accepts through Christ. The local church thus becomes a community of people who live for different purposes than the world, a community that experiences even from this age, imperfectly yet genuinely, the life of the world to come. And among the spiritual sacrifices offered by all Christians, since they are all (without exception) royal priests, what stands out is the proclamation of the excellencies of Him who called them out of darkness into His marvelous light (1 Pet. 2:1-9). And as the Church proclaims the virtues of the Triune God (which especially shine forth in the Gospel of Grace), the LORD continues to expand His spiritual kingdom.

The Epistles—growing deeper in the importance of the Gospel

The Gospels describe the events of Jesus' earthly life, focusing particularly on His crucifixion and resurrection. The *Epistles* (i.e., letters sent to the local churches) *expand* on the meaning of these events and the consequences that stem from them. Hence, they *focus* on the identity of Jesus, that he is the LORD (YHWH), as we have already seen; in what He did, that is, in the Good News; and in the new life that springs from our faith-union with Christ. Everything revolves around the Gospel. This is because the Good News is not useful just for the beginning of the Christian life. It is not something we learn to later move on to greener pastures. *The Good News is the foundation of the entire Christian life.* There is nothing of worth beyond the Good News. There is only a greater and deeper understanding of the unsearchable riches of Christ, which are seen in the inexhaustible beauty of the Gospel (Gal. 3:1-5).

The value and absolute centrality of the Gospel is evident from the apostle Paul's insistence on it. In every problem that afflicts the various local churches, whether it is divisions and strife or cases of sexual immorality, Paul's answer is to delve deeper into the Gospel with his Epistles and show how the solution lies in it—how everything relates to the cross of Christ.

Writing to the Corinthians, Paul emphatically states, ***"… I decided to know nothing among you except Jesus Christ and him crucified"*** (1 Cor. 2:2, emphasis mine). In the same epistle, Paul often puts this principle into practice. In the sixth chapter, he gives his answer to some of the Corinthians who were in danger of being carried away by Corinth's sinful culture. The society of that time was immersed in all forms of sexual immorality, like our modern western societies. And Paul, faced with such debauchery, commands, *"Flee from sexual immorality"* (1 Cor. 6:18a—the older English translations render the Greek word for sexual immorality as "fornication" since the Greek word *"porneia"* includes all kinds of sexual relationships outside marriage). Flee, says Paul, for the Holy Spirit indwells you, therefore your body is a temple of the Holy Spirit, and you are not your own. Indeed, he goes on to say that, *"You* *are not your own, for you were bought with a price. So glorify God in your body"* (1 Cor. 6:19b-20). Here is Paul's answer to the Corinthians' moral failures—Jesus Christ bought you with His blood (cf. Acts 20:28; 1 Pet. 1:18-19) and you belong to Him, therefore live for Him.

Paul has one purpose—to "present everyone mature in Christ" (Col. 1:28b). And to achieve this, at every opportunity and with all his energy, Paul says, *"[Jesus] we proclaim, warning everyone and teaching everyone …"* (Col. 1:28, emphasis mine). For Christ is enough. For in Christ *"… are hidden all the treasures of wisdom and knowledge"* (Col. 2:3). For whoever has Christ is complete in Him (Col. 2:10).

The apostle Paul insists so much on the gospel because he knows that *"… it is the power of God for salvation to everyone who believes …"* (Rom. 1:16). He knows this truth first-hand, as he himself experienced the transformative power of Christ. Paul was a Pharisee, a zealot, and a persecutor of Christ's disciples. This was the case because he could not accept that Jesus was the Messiah since He had died accursed on a cross. Not only that, but *Paul was* also *the definition of a legalist.* In other words, he thought that if he kept the law well enough, God would accept him. He trusted in himself, he considered himself to be "blameless" in terms of the righteousness that comes from law-keeping (Phil. 3:1-9). And so, he could not discern his need for Jesus until the risen Christ manifested Himself to Paul while he was on his way to Damascus to arrest the Christians there (Acts 9). As a result of this divine meeting, the former persecutor of Christ became the apostle to the Gentiles.

So Paul had every reason to be *thrilled* with the Gospel, with the free grace that Christ showed him. And until the end of his life, he never got over the fact that Christ chose him, saved him, and took him into His service, whereas until then he was His enemy. And so, at every opportunity, he declared that *"… Christ Jesus came into the world to save sinners, of whom I am the foremost"* (1 Tim. 1:15b). Paul, until Christ met him, was a legalist and relied on the observance of the law, that is, on what he himself did or did not do. Now he counts whatever gain he had as loss for the sake of Christ because he comprehends that the thing of supreme importance is to know Christ. And, while he trusted in his own righteousness in the past, now Paul trusts in Christ alone, in the righteousness of Christ alone, which God bestows through faith alone:

*"Indeed, I count everything as loss because of the surpassing worth of knowing Christ Jesus my Lord. For his sake I have suffered the loss of all things and count them as rubbish, in order that I may gain Christ and be found in him, **not having a righteousness of my own** that comes from the law, **but** that which comes through faith in Christ, **the righteousness from God that depends on faith** ... "* (Phil. 3:8-9, emphasis mine).

Christ is truly sufficient

Paul had truly experienced the greatness of Christ's free grace (Rom. 3:23-28; Eph. 2:8-9; Gal. 2:16). Having personally appropriated the beauty, power, and sufficiency of the Gospel, Paul had this great concern—not to allow the Gospel to be perverted, not to let people get misled into thinking that Christ is not enough. The same danger that existed then, of distorting the gospel of Christ's free grace, exists today. Therefore, *let us look at Paul's reasoning* in the Epistle to the Galatians, as he defends the Gospel against the poison of legalism.

Paul had preached the Gospel in the area of Galatia and churches had been formed, comprising of those who had received the Good News. However, soon enough false teachers, "false brothers" as Paul calls them (Gal. 2:4), tried to distort the Gospel of Christ's grace (Gal. 1:6-9) by arguing that for a man to be saved it is not enough to believe in Christ, but that he must keep the law also (Gal 2:16, 21, 3:21, 4:21, 5:1-4; cf. Acts 15:1, 5). And Paul, angry and saddened in his heart, writes the epistle to the Galatians (around 50 AD) in a polemic tone. He does not write a dry, theoretical dissertation. He writes with passion, aiming to protect the people of Galatia and, by extension, every Christian from the terrible danger of legalism. He strives so that the Gospel will remain unadulterated, for what is at *stake* is nothing less than our eternal future. Everything he writes in this letter is intended to support his central thesis:

> "... *yet we know that a person is not justified by works of the law but through faith in Jesus Christ, so* **we also have believed in Christ Jesus, in order to be justified by faith in Christ and not by works of the law,** *because by works of the law no one will be justified*" (Gal. 2:16, emphasis mine).

Paul's central argument is that no one can be justified by keeping the law (since the law requires perfect obedience—cf. Deut. 27:26 with Gal. 3:10). If anyone could have achieved this, then Christ would not have to die. Those who, therefore, try to be justified by the law, that is, by their obedient works, deny the grace of God (Gal. 2:21). They refuse to trust solely in the LORD Jesus. As a result, no matter what they claim about themselves, they remain under the curse of the law. As Paul writes, *"For* **all who rely on works of the law are under a curse;** *for it is written, 'Cursed be everyone who does not abide by all things written in the Book of the Law, and do them'"* (Gal. 3:10, emphasis mine).

How can one escape the curse of the law, i.e., the punishment that the law demands for every transgression? What is the alternative to the required personal, perfect, and perpetual obedience? To trust in the work of another. The only viable alternative is to trust in Him who took our place to redeem us with His blood from the curse of the law: **"Christ redeemed us from the curse of the law by becoming a curse for us**—*for it is written, 'Cursed is everyone who is hanged on a tree' ..."* (Gal. 3:13, emphasis mine).

The OT (Deut. 21:23) recorded the truth that whoever dies hanged on a tree is cursed by God. And Christ on the cross fulfilled these words literally; He died condemned and accursed, having become a curse and sin for us. And so, He redeemed us with His precious blood, as the curse of the law fell upon Him.

When Adam disobeyed and turned against the LORD, he found

himself under the curse of the law. One of the consequences of his fall was that this curse would also affect the rest of physical creation. We know this, for the LORD, on that terrible day, said to Adam, *"... **cursed is the ground because of you;** in pain you shall eat of it all the days of your life; **thorns** and thistles it shall bring forth for you ... "* (Gen. 3:17b-18, emphasis mine). These *thorns* were the visible symbol of the curse that fell on humankind because of the sin of Adam. This symbol was placed on the head of Jesus, as He was dying on the cross. The crown of *thorns* that the Romans fastened to the head of Jesus displays what truly happened on the cross. There, Jesus was hanged on the tree, lifting upon Himself our own curse.

Jesus did all this as the last Adam. The NT Scriptures use this analogy (Rom. 5:14; 1 Cor. 15:20-22, 45-49). The first Adam was obligated to fulfill the requirements of the law, representing all humankind. These requirements were twofold: perfect obedience and punishment for every transgression. *Christ, the descendant of Eve, came to the world and became the last Adam.* He became like us to succeed where the first one failed—the LORD came to fulfill all the requirements of the law on behalf of His people.

The law, firstly, requires perfect obedience. And so, *"in the fullness of time,"* Jesus was sent by the Father to be born *"under the law, to redeem those who were under the law"* (Gal. 4:4b-5a). Jesus obeyed the law perfectly throughout His earthly life; not for Himself but in the place of every one of His people. And this obedience, this righteousness, Jesus bestows *as a gift* to everyone who genuinely trusts Him (Rom. 5:17-19).

The law, secondly, requires punishment for every transgression. The LORD fulfilled this requirement also, as He paid the cost with His own blood on the cross, becoming a curse for us.

Before we did anything, we were condemned in the person of our representative, Adam. Before we did anything, Jesus fulfilled the requirements of the law, and He now bestows His righteousness (truly, Jesus is "The LORD, our righteousness"—Jer. 23:6) to all those who trust In

Him: *"For as by the one man's disobedience the many were made sinners, so by the one man's obedience **the many will be made righteous**"* (Rom. 5:19, emphasis mine).

Jesus lived the life we had to live and tasted the death penalty we deserved. In this way, He redeemed from the curse of the law all those who trust Him. *And this is why those who genuinely trust in Christ are no longer under the law but under grace* (Rom. 6:14).

Paul insists with all his might (he even argued publicly with the apostle Peter when Peter contradicted the Gospel with his behavior—Gal. 2:10-14) that man is saved solely by faith in Christ alone *to make very clear that Christ is truly enough, i.e., that everything a sinful man needs is found in the Savior.* This is the point of *crucial* importance. This is the point that makes the *difference* between eternal life and eternal death.

Unfortunately, many religious people who claim to be Christians disagree that faith in Christ is sufficient. They perhaps do not realize that, by denying that faith in Christ is enough for salvation, they end up denying that Christ Himself is sufficient. This is the case because only one of the two following propositions can be true: *either* all that is necessary for our salvation is *not* found in Jesus Christ, *or* if *all* things necessary are in Christ, then those who receive Christ through faith alone *have perfect salvation being united with Him.*

To such religious people, the apostle Paul addresses *a very stern warning:* *"You are severed from Christ, you who would be justified by the law; you have fallen away from grace"* (Gal. 5:4). How dreadful. Those people who say they believe in Christ, but at the same time base their standing with God on their law-keeping, have severed themselves from Christ since they deny His grace.

This interpretation of God's grace in the Epistle to the Galatians is found not only in the writings of, say, Luther, but even in the works of the early church's theologians. One such *example* can be found in the book with interpretive comments on the Epistle to the Galatians written by Marius Victorinus.[30]

One of the most characteristic excerpts of this book, an excerpt expressing the spirit of the entire commentary, is the following, which we find in the comments concerning Galatians 5:9 (italics mine):

> Your supposed little bit that you have added—namely, that you would observe circumcision and other things—that little bit of yours, since it is spoiled, spoils the mass of our gospel. The result is that your full hope is not invested in Christ, and Christ does not regard you as his own, as people who have their hope from him. For faith liberates, and *anyone, as we have said, who hopes for help in any way besides Christ, even if it be along with Christ, does not have faith.*[31]

Victorinus is clear: if someone tries to add anything to faith in Christ, literally anything, then that "faith" turns out to be false. *These words are truly terrifying* for those who recognize themselves in this description. Even if you claim to belong to Christ but you hope in anything else along with Christ, then Christ will not benefit you at all because you have no faith, and thus you are lost away from Him.

Dear reader, if your hope is in churches, ceremonies, sacraments, people (living or dead), or in what you do or do not do, Christ will not benefit you at all. *I plead with you with all my heart—repent and trust solely in the LORD Jesus Christ.*

The newness of life in Christ

As we have seen, the LORD Jesus redeemed His people through His shed blood on the cross, i.e., He achieved for them the forgiveness of their sins: *"In [Christ] we have **redemption** through his blood, **the forgiveness of our trespasses,** according to the riches of his grace"* (Eph. 1:7, emphasis mine). This forgiveness is received solely through faith in Christ alone. For this reason, when the jailer at Philippi asked the apostle Paul what he must do to be saved, Paul answered, *"**Believe in the Lord Jesus Christ, and you will be saved** ..."* (Acts 16:30-31, emphasis mine).

At the same time, it is worth emphasizing that whoever trusts in Christ alone for salvation *receives new life* as he is born again to a living hope

(1 Pet. 1:3) because, by faith, he has been united with the One who *is eternal life* (1 John 5:12-13, 20). *The truth is that we do not add Jesus to our life; we receive Him as our life* because we have no true life until He meets us by His Spirit. And when one obtains this new, genuine life, he begins to live differently. This *transformed life is the outward proof of the authenticity of faith;* it is the proof of one's encounter with the living Christ. One cannot come to know the LORD personally and yet remain unchanged.

Paul describes the fruit of salvation as follows: *"For we are his work-manship,* **created in Christ Jesus for good works,** *which God prepared beforehand, that we should walk in them"* (Eph. 2:10, emphasis mine). Everyone who, having been saved by grace alone through faith alone, has become a new creation (Eph. 2:1-9) will, *as a result,* walk in the good works that God has prepared for him. Certainly, he will not live perfectly since perpetual, sinless perfection will only be an experiential reality in the new heavens and earth. He will, however, live differently from those who do not belong to Christ. For Christ is the great Savior who graciously gives *both justification* (salvation from the guilt of sin) *and sanctification* (salvation from the bondage of sin)—known in re-formed theology as *Christ's double benefit.*

Concerning this *twofold grace,* Peter writes, *"... who Himself [Jesus] bore our sins in His own body on the tree, that we,* **having died to sins, might live for righteousness**—*by whose stripes you were healed. For you were like sheep going astray, but have now returned to the Shepherd and Overseer of your souls"* (1 Pet. 2:24-25 NKJV, emphasis mine). Christ bore our sins in His body on the tree so that now, being forgiven and having died to sins, we should live for righteousness. *And this is because those who hear the greatest story and meet its Hero through faith are incorporated into Him.* They identify with Him. They participate, united with Him, in His death and resurrection (Rom. 6:1-11; Gal. 2:20; Eph. 2:1-10). And thus, they die as to what they were until then (slaves to sin, as Peter writes, *"... having died to sins"*—1 Pet. 2:24) and are *resurrected* in newness of life *("to live for righteousness").*

As we have seen, this new life is given by Christ as *a free gift* to every sinner who trusts Him. At the same time, the truth is that this *resurrection* presupposes death to sin. And this is the main reason why people deny Christ: they are evil, love sin, and do not want to forsake it. They do not want to be freed from their shackles. And that is why Christ's call seems painful to them (as every death is); their hands are filled with the rubbish of sin, and they are not willing to throw it away to, empty-handed, receive Christ for all that He is.

But *the only way* to receive Christ *is empty-handed,* with the realization that He is more worthy than anything and anyone else, with the confession that no one and nothing else can be compared to Him. He Himself thus defines the attitude man must have in order to approach Him truly. In the fourteenth chapter of the Gospel according to Luke, *the LORD declares* to the crowd that follows Him *that for someone to be His disciple* (in other words, to begin the Christian life) one *must*: love Christ more than all his relatives, even his own life (Luke 14:26; cf. Matt. 10:37-39); die to his ambitions and be willing to live as the LORD wills, whatever the cost may be (14:27); and be ready to renounce all his possessions (14:33). In short, what marks the man who comes to Christ with genuine faith is his willingness and desire to cease worshipping the gifts of Christ (that is, all kinds of created goods) and from now on to love, worship, obey, and thank above all else the Giver of all these gifts.

We conclude that one must first have his eyes opened to see the truth in order to receive Christ and all His gracious benefits. That is, to see that Christ is infinitely precious¬. Until this happens, the commandments of Christ will seem burdensome to the unbeliever, and he will continue in his love of sin, which keeps him away from Christ. When a man's eyes are opened to the glorious majesty of Christ, then his hands are opened as well, idols previously held fast fall to the ground, and *empty-handedly he receives Christ to be his treasure.*

Jesus likens His kingdom and Himself to a treasure hidden in a field, which, when one finds it, sells all that He has *with immense joy* to buy that field (Matt. 13:44). This man will certainly be mocked by his neighbors; they will call him a fool. He, however, does not care about other people's opinions anymore. And he does not think he is making any sacrifices. He sells everything, but, as Jesus says in the parable, he does it with joy, for he has found a great treasure. The treasure who is more precious than everything else and whom he receives with *empty hands.*

Empty hands, firstly, because we have absolutely nothing to offer Him, nothing to present to deserve His acceptance. *Empty hands, secondly,* because we now trust Him to be the source of our joy, peace, and security, instead of all that we had held tightly in our embrace. In this manner, Jesus reinstates His rightful place in our life. Of course, the only place that befits Him is the center. As in a solar system, where only if the sun is at its center will the planets have the correct orbit, so in our lives, only if Christ is at the center, only if Christ is the treasure of our soul, will the various areas of our life find and stay in their proper place.

The new life that the LORD Jesus gives us commences when we receive Him *empty-handedly.* As already stated, this life is marked by love for the LORD, which is our response to His love that compels us to live for Him who for our sake died and was raised (2 Cor. 5:14-15). From this love springs forth genuine evangelical obedience (John 14:15, 21, 23) since, for those who genuinely believe in Christ, God's commandments are not burdensome (1 John 5:1-5).

The key to progress in this new life is growing in the grace and knowledge of Christ. The more I come to know Him, the more I love Him, and the more I become like Him and follow Him. The more I understand who I am *already* in Christ (i.e., what is the identity that Christ has *already* given me), the more I will have the will and strength to live in such a way as to please God.

This key marks the structure of Paul's epistles. He never begins by issuing commandments. God's commandments are holy, just, and good, but in and of themselves, cannot give us the strength we need to obey them. Paul always starts his letters by proclaiming how wonderful the LORD is and how precious and perfect His salvation is. And only after having first explained what the position of all who are in Christ is and what is already true of them in light of the Gospel does he proceed to the hortatory part of his epistles, in which he describes the morality of this new life. He does that because the strength we need to walk in this new, supernatural life is found *only* in the Gospel of Christ.

All the commandments we find in the writings of the NT Scriptures are based on the Gospel. (One such example is located in Colossians 3:1-4, where Paul declares: you have already been raised with Christ, your life is hidden with Christ in God—the indicative part. *Therefore* now *"set your minds on things above"* and live accordingly—Col. 3:5-17, the imperative part.) Everywhere we find the same pattern: you are *already* new in Christ; *live out what you already are.* Christian, know how rich you are in Christ, and live accordingly.

The more we are assured of Christ's love for us, the more our hearts are filled with gratitude, and we become "heartily willing and ready henceforth to live unto Him." And so, we are able to live and finally die *with the joy of the* comfort *that only Christ gives.* This comfort, which is *the only one* that can persevere not only in every circumstance of life but even in the face of death, is described beautifully and warmly in the first question and answer of the Heidelberg Catechism:

Question 1. What is thy only comfort in life and in death?[32]
Answer: That I, with body and soul, both in life and in death, am not my own, but belong to my faithful Saviour Jesus Christ, who with His precious blood has fully satisfied for all my sins, and redeemed me from all the power of the devil; and so preserves me, that without the will of my Father in heaven not a hair can fall from my head; yea, that all things must work together for my salvation. Wherefore, by His Holy Spirit, He also assures me of eternal life, and makes me heartily willing and ready henceforth to live unto Him.

And as we live for Christ, we should never forget how wonderful it is that we can please our loving Father with our imperfect works. And it is wonderful, for nothing less than absolute perfection can stand before the perfect Judge. Our best deeds can never come close to this measure, as our motives are always mixed. And, consequently, on their own our works have no value. And yet, those who belong to the LORD Jesus do not have God against them as a Judge, but the Father of Christ has also become their own compassionate Father. We can, therefore, please Him as we live by faith, for the Father receives us, being united with Christ through faith, and at the same time, He receives our imperfect works through Jesus also. Like the parents of a five-year-old child rejoice when she presents them with an incomplete painting, so also our heavenly Father rejoices when He sees us walking in the good works He has prepared for us (all the while working in us that which pleases Him through Jesus—Heb. 13:21). Let us please Him, then, by living with faith (Heb. 11:6) as we remember that even for a cup of cold water which we will give in the name of Christ, we will not lose the reward, which God will graciously give us (Mark 9:41).

* * *

As Jonathan Gibson so eloquently stated, the greatest story reveals:

> "... the Warrior-Son who comes to earth to slay his enemy and rescue his Father's people. Christ is the Good Shepherd who lays down his life for his sheep, a loving Bridegroom who gives himself for his bride, and a victorious King who lavishes the spoils of his conquest on the citizens of his realm. He is the Head who sacrifices himself for the body, the Master who dies for his friends, the Firstborn who gives himself for his brothers and sisters, the Last Adam who falls into a deep sleep and from his riven side, as with the first Adam, comes his bride."[33]

Blessed is the man
who trusts in the LORD,
and whose hope is the LORD.

Jeremiah 17:7

Our Response to the Savior

Given all we have explored thus far, it becomes evident what the LORD requires of us in response to all He has done—He invites us to *trust in Him*. Adam and Eve (and all their descendants after them) turned away from Christ and despised Him by declaring with their actions that Jesus was not enough; they refused to trust in Him. The solution is to reverse this attitude, which is exactly what *the LORD asks of us*—to recognize that He is supremely worthy and receive Him as the ultimate treasure He is, *returning to Him with simple, humble faith.*

Simple faith, hearty trust in the Person and work of Christ, is the only reasonable response to His call. *The Gospel calls man to believe in Christ to be saved.* However, this saving faith is not a mere intellectual understanding and assent to the contents of the Gospel; assent is necessary, but it is not enough. It is not enough to agree that Christ is the Savior of sinners who was delivered for our trespasses and raised for our justification and that He alone is the way, and the truth, and the life. *What marks genuine faith is the personal relationship of trust with the risen and living LORD Jesus.* The man who genuinely believes in Christ receives Him as his righteousness, his treasure, his life, and his all.

Many people claim to believe in God, meaning that they merely acknowledge His existence. But the essence of true faith is hearty, humble trust in Christ, dependence on the LORD Jesus alone. The Heidelberg Catechism's *definition* of true faith is as follows:

Question 21. What is true faith?[34]
Answer: True faith is not only a certain knowledge whereby I hold for truth all that God has revealed to us in His Word; but also a

hearty trust, which the Holy Ghost works in me by the Gospel, that not only to others, but to me also, forgiveness of sins, everlasting righteousness and salvation are freely given by God, merely of grace, only for the sake of Christ's merits.

* * *

Space limitations prevent an exhaustive study of every biblical scene revealing Christ. The entire Bible bears witness to Him, and the Bible is a big book (in fact, it is a library consisting of sixty-six books). Therefore, we will conclude this section *with three more OT pictures that confirm what we have said about the response the Savior expects from us and the nature of true faith.* These images *reveal* (a) the absolute sufficiency of Christ's work that requires no addition on our part; (b) His gracious bestowal of all things as a free gift to His own; and (c) the nature of true, saving faith through which sinful man receives the Savior and becomes one with Him.

(a) *Let us look at the scene of David's battle with Goliath* (1 Sam. 17). The anointed shepherd-king *fights against Goliath,* the enemy of God, *on behalf* of all the Israelites. The result of this duel will decide the outcome of the entire battle, as the two armies will not participate. Indeed, David crushed the Philistines by defeating Goliath, their champion. *Likewise, Jesus, the descendant of David, represented His people as their great Champion.* On the cross He was victorious for them, defeating the devil with his own weapon. He crushed the ancient serpent on the Cross, for the devil's weapon is death (Heb. 2:14-18), and the death of Christ marked the death of death. Death tried to swallow Life, and Life swallowed death. While His people were utterly incapable of doing anything to help themselves, the *LORD Jesus did it all in their place,* and now He gives them His victory. Sharing in His triumph, we may also march with joy like the Israelites did when they saw David raise the enemy's severed head before them.

(b) *Let us look at the sacrifices of animals and their typology.* Under the Mosaic law, the Israelite who sinned had to confess his sin before the priest, lay his hands on the head of the animal that was to be sacrificed to transfer his guilt to it, and *the animal would die in his place* (Lev. 1:1-5, 5:5-6, 16:21). The believing Israelites knew that these sacrifices and the Levitical priesthood could *not* achieve forgiveness. They reminded them of their sinfulness and of the coming Messiah, the Messiah who would come to represent them, *substitute them, and sacrifice Himself in their place* to grant them the forgiveness of sins once and for all, as a free gift. Today, we look by faith and confess our sins to the only and eternal High Priest, Jesus. There is no group of special priests (*all* Christians are priests of the great King—1 Pet. 2:9), there are no "sacraments," no church can save, and there is no other mediator between God and men but the man Christ Jesus (1 Tim. 2:5).

(c) *Let us look at the scene where the bronze snake was set up in the wilderness.* This is perhaps the most illuminating image concerning *the nature of true, saving faith* (cf. Num. 21:4-9 with John 3:14-16). The Israelites speak against the LORD sometime after He has taken them out of the land of slavery. They go as far as to say that they were better off in Egypt. And the LORD sends venomous serpents to bite them as punishment for their sin. Therefore, the Israelites are bitten and die one after another. Recognizing their sin, they plead with Moses to intercede on their behalf. And the LORD says to Moses: make a bronze serpent, set it on a pole, and tell the Israelites, "*... everyone who is bitten, when he sees it, shall live*" (Num. 21:5-9). Indeed, Moses obeys the command of the LORD and half-dead Israelites who believe the *promise* of God *look to the bronze snake and live.* Using this incident as a teaching aid, Jesus said, "*... as Moses lifted up the serpent in the wilderness, so must the Son of Man be lifted up,* **that whoever believes in him may have eternal life**" (John 3:14-15, emphasis mine). He must be lifted up so that everyone who understands he has been bitten by sin and believes the *promise* of Jesus who was lifted up on the cross (that is, *looks* with faith to the crucified Savior) may be saved. *A believing look to the Cross is* *enough for sinful man to be saved,* to find perfect forgiveness, and receive new, eternal life—life that begins there and then and will last forever.

Faith, genuine faith that looks solely to Christ, is the only means, only channel, and only instrument through which we receive Him and the salvation He freely gives (Eph. 2:8-9; John 1:12). All Scripture proclaims: *Look to Jesus and you will live;* look to *Him alone.* Therefore, fix your eyes on Jesus, dear reader, and keep looking unto Him, regardless of your circumstances, as the author of Hebrews exhorts us: *"... let us run with endurance the race that is set before us, looking to Jesus ..."* (Heb. 12:1b-2a).

Look:

- BACK, two thousand years ago, to the cross and the empty tomb; for the Crucifixion and Resurrection of the LORD is the most significant and world-changing event in all of human history. It is the event that gives meaning to everything. It is the event to which we owe everything, as every good thing we receive flows from that Cross. Look to the tree (illumined by the resurrection) where your Savior, *"... for the joy that was set before him endured the cross, despising the shame ..."* (Heb. 12:2).
- UP, toward heaven, where the risen LORD, your own High Priest, is seated on the throne and presently intercedes for you, showing the scars of His sacrifice before the Father (Heb. 7:24-25). Look, and draw near to the throne of grace with the confidence the great High Priest gives you, to *"... receive mercy and find grace to help in time of need"* (Heb. 4:14-16).
- FORWARD, toward the finish line, where the LORD Jesus awaits to welcome you into His immediate presence. He beckons you onward, urging you to keep your gaze steadfast upon Him until the day He raises you into His eternal kingdom.

Look to Him who suffered and was resurrected from the dead on the third day, "according to the Scriptures," so that repentance and forgiveness of sins should be proclaimed in His name to all nations. Look to Him who, seated on the heavenly throne, reigns. Look to Him who "*is coming soon.*" Look to Christ, for He Himself asks you to do so through the prophet Isaiah: "'**Look to Me, and be saved,** *all you ends of the earth! For I am God, and there is no other*'" (Isa. 45:22 NKJV, emphasis mine). And live by faith in Him. Live with Him while waiting for the heavenly city that the LORD is preparing for those who love Him.

* * *

We saw the LORD, the great Redeemer, accomplish everything necessary to redeem His people from their sins once and for all. By His blood, He redeemed all who trust in Him from the *guilt* of sin and is constantly delivering them from its *power.* And one day, He will fully liberate His people even from the *presence* of sin when He will bring them into His eternal kingdom, where His righteousness dwells.

We will now turn our attention to the heavenly city, the new heaven and the new earth that the LORD will usher in at His second coming, as we will study the last chapter of the greatest story, the chapter of the Final Restoration of all things.

Of this I am sure. If salvation is not all of grace, I will not be saved. If any aspect of salvation is dependent upon me doing or not doing something, I will not be in heaven. If what Christ did alone is not enough to make me just before God, I will be in hell.

Todd Nibert

We live between two great days:
the day Christ hung before men
and the day all men will kneel
before Christ.

Paul Washer

I would not give one moment of heaven for all the
joy and riches of the world, even if it lasted for
thousands and thousands of years.

Martin Luther

I bear my testimony that there is no joy to be found in all this world like that of sweet communion with Christ. I would barter all else there is of heaven for that. Indeed, that is heaven.

C. H. Spurgeon

But our citizenship is in heaven,
and from it we await a Savior,
the Lord Jesus Christ ...

Philippians 3:20

Your eyes will behold the
king in his beauty; they will
see a land that stretches afar.

Isaiah 33:17

You make known to me the path of life;
in your presence there is fullness of joy;
at your right hand are pleasures forevermore

Psalm 16:11

Then I saw a new heaven
and a new earth, for the first heaven
and the first earth had passed away ...

Revelation 21:1

4. FINAL RESTORATION

The day of Jesus' second coming

In the NT Scriptures, we frequently find the promise that the LORD is coming soon, that He comes triumphant. Unlike other religions and philosophies, Christianity proclaims that human history is heading toward a specific goal: *toward the LORD Jesus' second coming.* And then, this world in its present form will end.

In His second coming, Christ will come in His glory with all His angels, and, before Him, *"every knee should bow"* and *"every tongue confess that Jesus Christ is Lord, to the glory of God the Father"* (Phil. 2:10-11). On that day, the LORD will judge "the living and the dead." He will come to put an end to all this wickedness that now seems so dominant around us. He will come to deliver perfect justice.

This will be a day of judgment and eternal condemnation for all sinners who remained away from Christ. Unbelievers who will then be alive and the unbelieving dead, who will come out of the tombs to the *"resurrection of judgment"* (John 5:28-29), *will meet Christ as their Judge.* All their deeds will be made manifest, they will be *judged according to their evil deeds,* and they will get what they deserve. They will be thrown into the eternal lake of fire (Rev. 20:11-15), along with the devil and all his minions. The magnitude of the punishment reveals how much sin offends the infinite and holy God; it shows the seriousness of the crime. This will be the final victory of the great Warrior against His enemy—the ancient serpent will be tormented in hell forever.

On the other hand, that day, the day of the LORD, will be a day of joy and perfect salvation for all who belong to Christ. *They will meet Him as their Savior and Friend.* This day is awaited by all believers, those on earth today, and those who died believing in Christ. Believers who have died are in an *intermediate state*. Their souls have been separated from their bodies, and they are consciously (now, at this moment) in the immediate presence of the LORD and enjoy the company of the Lamb who was slain. This is the clear teaching of Scripture. Let us remember the thief who was crucified next to Jesus. When he understood who it was that hung by his side, he pleaded with the LORD to remember him when He would come into His kingdom, with Christ replying, *"Truly, I say to you, today you will be with me in paradise"* (Luke 23:39-43). By His grace, Christ saved this justly convicted criminal. And also, let us remember Paul's anticipation and certainty that, when he departs from this world, he will be with Christ, which is far better (Phil. 1:20-25). Finally, let us note the picture we find in Revelation, where believers who have lost their lives because of their faith in Christ are currently in heaven and ask Him to "avenge their blood" (Rev. 6:9-11).

Believers, therefore, who have died in Christ (i.e., died believing in Christ) currently participate in heavenly worship (Rev. 5) and look forward to that day, the day of *final redemption*. That is when the resurrection of the dead will take place. Believers who will be alive on earth that day will be transformed in the blink of an eye, clothed in incorruptibility and immortality (1 Cor. 15). Believers who have died will come out of the tombs in the "resurrection of life" (John 5:28-29); their souls will be reunited with their new, glorified bodies. The fact that believers, at the time of the resurrection, will immediately be given their new spiritual body proves that they will not face condemnation (John 5:24). They are *already* righteous in Christ. They are accepted because their name is written in "the book of life of the Lamb who was slain" (Rev. 20:11-15, 13:8, 17:8). This book contains the names of all those that Christ, the slain Lamb, ransomed for God by His precious blood on the cross (Rev. 5:9). *Thus, believers will be ultimately received by God exclusively because of the work of Christ on their behalf.* Their good works are not in any way the reason they will be admitted to the new heavens and earth. Their deeds, especially their practical love for other Christians, the brothers and sisters of Christ (cf. Matt. 25:31-46 with Matt. 12:50, 28:10), will simply serve as public evidence to the genuineness of their faith.

On that day, all the people of God, the whole body of Christ, His genuine church, will participate in the astounding miracle of the *final restoration,* when everything will become completely new (see the last two chapters of Revelation). Then, all believers (who collectively form the bride of Christ) will meet the LORD in the air and be with Him forever (1 Thess. 4:17). Who can imagine how magnificent His second coming will be?

On that day, all Christians will see Christ face to face and shall be like Him (1 John 3:1-2). We will have a glorious and immortal body like His since the LORD, after His resurrection and ascension, did not throw away His human nature (Phil. 3:20-21). We will be given new, perfected hearts, perfectly restored minds, new eyes suited to see His glory, and loud voices to praise the wonderful LORD—the LORD who used His almighty power to redeem us with His blood and prepare for us this amazing future. And, together with us, the entire creation will be delivered from futility and corruption (Rom. 8:18-23).

Who can imagine how amazing the new heaven and the new earth the LORD Jesus is preparing for those who love Him will be? Who can imagine the moment of the enthronement of the Lamb when, having triumphed over all His enemies, He will return to His throne with all His people? David prophetically describes this beautiful scene: *"Lift up your heads, O you gates! And be lifted up, you **everlasting doors! And the King of glory shall come in.** Who is this King of glory? The LORD strong and mighty, the LORD mighty in battle"* (Ps. 24:7-8 NKJV, emphasis mine). The great victor, the King of glory, the LORD of hosts, simultaneously with all His people, passes through the eternal doors and enters the heavenly city. The One who once had a crown of thorns put on His head now comes to His enthronement, with myriads of myriad angels around Him and the countless multitude of the redeemed crying out with a loud voice, saying, *"Salvation belongs to our God who sits on the throne, and to the Lamb!"* (Rev. 7:10).

What about you, dear reader? Do you want to be *there?*

Do you know if you will be *there?* Do you long for that day?

There, pain, sorrow, loneliness, disease, death, fear, and sin shall be no more. *There,* at last, we will be free even from the presence of corruption both in our hearts and in our environment. We will be free from all sickness and weakness, and God will wipe away all tears from our eyes. *There,* we will finally be able to love Him endlessly with all our heart, soul, mind, and strength. And at last, *there,* we will be able to enjoy the infinite joy of Christ's presence perfectly and the eternal pleasures found in Him, individually and together as one body. Forever!

We don't have much information about the new heavens and earth, nor do we know what abilities our resurrected bodies will have. There will be continuity with the present condition but also discontinuity. It is like a seed that falls to the earth, dies, and then a large tree grows (1 Cor. 15:35-49). There is a kind of continuity, but if someone who does not know how plants grow were to learn that a whole tree came out of a seed, he would be astonished. That's how it is with the new heavens and the new earth. Perhaps we are not given more details¬ because, quite simply, the re-created world will be so superior to the present one that, even if God revealed them to us now, we would not be able to understand them. Maybe. What is certain, however, is that God does not give us more details so as not to get confused and end up focusing on that which is secondary. *Heaven is heaven because the LORD Jesus is there.* And that is more than enough. Paradise is paradise because the LORD is there. He is our paradise, He is our life, He is our all in all. God wants us to keep *looking* to His Son and our eternal future with Him as we progress through this world's wilderness toward our heavenly homeland.

Eternity and the institutions of the Sabbath and Marriage

Let us *look,* then, to Jesus and the new heavens and earth by exploring two symbolic pictures (types), which aim to illuminate the *eternal future* which Christ is preparing for everyone who belongs to Him. These pictures, which we encounter even from the very beginning of creation, are:

(a) the Sabbath
(b) the institution of Marriage.

(a) We first meet the idea of the Sabbath in the second chapter of Genesis (2:2-3). The Hebrew word "sabbath" (translated as the number "seven") sounds remarkably similar to the Hebrew verb translated as "to cease / to rest." And indeed, God blessed the seventh day and made it holy because He completed all His creative work and "rested' on it. Of course, He does not need rest; but we do. And the first people were created on the sixth day; therefore, the first full day of their lives was the Sabbath, the day the LORD had blessed. After the fall of men, the LORD continued to care for them: He gave them one day each week to cease from all their work and toil. This day's purpose was for them to rest and enable them (and us) to look to God, the One who is the true rest, the true Sabbath. This is why the incarnate LORD Jesus invites people with the words *"Come to me, all who labor and are heavy laden, and **I will give you rest"*** (Matt. 11:28, emphasis mine).

Furthermore, the Sabbath day points us to the eternal rest that awaits those who trust in Christ (see Heb. 4). As we read in Revelation: *"... 'Blessed are the dead who die in the Lord from now on.' 'Blessed indeed,' says the Spirit, 'that they may rest from their labors ...'"* (Rev. 14:13).

The weekly day of rest is a small foretaste of the perfect rest that awaits those whom the LORD will resurrect in His immediate presence, in the new heaven and the new earth. Rest thus (this is the Sabbath's meaning for us) and Paradise go together. *Rest, therefore, is the first picture* that, even from the very beginning of creation, the Bible gives us to describe the coming Paradise.

Is this true of you, dear reader? Have you already entered this rest *solely by faith* in the LORD Jesus? God made us for Himself, and our heart is restless until it rests in Him, as Augustine once wrote.

(b) *The other picture* is the institution *of Marriage,* which we also find in the second chapter of Genesis (2:18-25). Marriage, a good gift God gave to people, has a deeper purpose: to display Christ's relationship with His bride, the Church (Eph. 5:22-33). If the Sabbath shows the rest that awaits God's people, *marriage displays the perfect unity and intimacy* that mark the loving relationship that believers in Christ will enjoy with Him in His immediate presence, in the new heavens and the new earth. And truly, the picture of a wedding is found in Revelation, the last book of the Bible, to describe Jesus' longed-for encounter with His people on that day:

> "'Let us rejoice and exult and give him the glory, for the marriage of the Lamb has come, and his Bride has made herself ready; it was granted her to clothe herself with fine linen, bright and pure'—for the fine linen is the righteous deeds of the saints. And the angel said to me, 'Write this: **Blessed are those who are invited to the marriage supper of the Lamb.'** And he said to me, 'These are the true words of God'" (Rev. 19:7-9, emphasis mine).

Then the LORD will see the radiant beauty of His bride, as she will perfectly reflect His own glory. And what will follow is an eternal, endless, incomparably incredible celebration. An enormous festival of everlasting joy awaits those who will be found at the marriage supper of the Lamb; absolute, unspeakable, inexpressible, glorious, ever-increasing joy in Christ's presence as He continuously reveals the inexhaustible aspects of His astonishing beauty. Indeed, the whole of eternity will not be enough to exhaust the beauty and majesty of Him who is eternally infinite and infinitely eternal!

These promises of perfect, eternal rest and intimate union with God in Christ in a fully restored creation are more than enough to satisfy the inquiries concerning eternity of all who genuinely love the LORD Jesus.

Knowledge of our eternal future changes our present

The precious truths concerning the eternal future the LORD is preparing for those who love Him have not been given just to gratify our curiosity. Every truth of Scripture is meant to transform us as it reveals Christ. By seeing with the eyes of faith the LORD Jesus and the inconceivable eternity that lies ahead for us with Him, the Holy Spirit changes our present. Our desires change, and thus, so do our priorities and choices. *And that is how the purpose and meaning of our lives change.*

The certainty of eternal life, that blessed assurance that the LORD bestows, is the catalyst for our hearts to break free from temporary, earthly goods and desires. Christians *"… seek the things that are above, where Christ is, seated at the right hand of God. **Set your minds on things that are above,** not on things that are on earth"* (Col. 3:1-2, emphasis mine). In this way, they are enabled to live for their Lord here and now. They remember that their labor for the LORD's sake is never in vain (1 Cor. 15:58).

As Christians remember this truth, they can endure persecution and all sorts of suffering and trials for Christ's sake. Just as the apostle Paul says about himself, *"So we do not lose heart. Though our outer self is wasting away, our inner self is being renewed day by day. For this light momentary affliction is preparing for us an eternal weight of glory beyond all comparison, **as we look not to the things that are seen but to the things that are unseen.** For the things that are seen are transient, but **the things that are unseen are eternal"*** (2 Cor. 4:16-18, emphasis mine).

The apostle Paul is repeatedly persecuted and tortured. It is no exaggeration to say that he suffers in every possible way for Christ's sake. He is imprisoned, whipped, stoned, shipwrecked, hungry, cold, sleepless, and anxious for the churches, yet he endures. His inner man is renewed as he gazes upon the eternal and consciously lives on the verge of eternity. And so he is able to conclude that all he is going through is a *"light momentary affliction"* compared to the *"eternal weight of glory"* that God has prepared for him.

We, too, can endure trials, disappointments, failures, sorrows, betrayals, envy, ingratitude, and rejection from other people as we *remember that one day we will inherit the entire universe with the LORD Jesus,* as the Bible promises: *"… and if children, then heirs—heirs of God and **fellow heirs with Christ,** provided we suffer with him in order that we may also be glorified with him"* (Rom. 8:17, emphasis mine).

The more Christians turn their attention to their eternal future, the more they are enabled to worship the LORD in their present, as the apostle John teaches: *"See what kind of love the Father has given to us, that we should be called children of God; and so we are. The reason why the world does not know us is that it did not know him. Beloved, we are God's children now, and what we will be has not yet appeared; but **we know** that when he appears we shall be like him, because we shall see him as he is. **And everyone who thus hopes in him purifies himself as he is pure"*** (1 John 3:1-3, emphasis mine).

The assurance God's genuine children have of this face-to-face encounter with Jesus does not lead them to indifference. On the contrary, as the apostle John affirms, whoever has the certain hope that he will one day see Jesus and be like Him purifies himself even from now, as he desires to resemble increasingly the One he worships. The more one focuses on his eternal future with Christ, the more Heaven's light shines upon his heart and, consequently, the more his life becomes fruitful, to the glory of his Savior.

* * *

The Spirit and the Bride say,
"Come."
And let the one who hears say,
"Come."
And let the one who is thirsty come;
let the one who desires take the water of life without price.

. . .

He who testifies to these things says,
"Surely I am coming soon."
Amen. Come, Lord Jesus!

Revelation 22:17, 20

INSTEAD OF AN EPILOGUE

INSTEAD OF AN EPILOGUE BECAUSE THIS STORY IS THE ONLY never-ending story. This story's closing chapter, which we just studied, will last for all eternity. Eternity is a concept that transcends us and simultaneously attracts us. For God has set the sense of eternity in our hearts. And this feeling, this need we have for something that transcends our finite minds, is a powerful indication that what we crave does exist. How can one describe the duration of eternity? In our perishable world, everything has a beginning and an end. What picture can give us even a foretaste of the state that is to come? We can imagine a huge granite boulder and a sparrow on the top of the rock, pecking at it with its beak. The "damage' that the sparrow does to the rock can, by analogy, be said to correspond to the first ten million years of the wondrous eternity that God has prepared for those who love Him. This is, then, why the last section of this book is titled "instead of an epilogue:" because there can be no epilogue to a story that will never end.

Instead of an epilogue because no one can get past this story and its importance in our quest to understand the world in which we live. What are the alternative options? Atheist author Richard Dawkins wrote:

> In a universe of blind physical forces and genetic replication, some people are going to get hurt, other people are going to get lucky, and you won't find any rhyme or reason in it, nor any justice. The universe we observe has precisely the properties we should expect if there is, at bottom, no design, no purpose, no evil and no good, nothing but blind, pitiless indifference.[35]

What depth of darkness. At the center of the universe for this man, there is nothing but blind, pitiless indifference. A worldview, then, which, starting from the axiom that there is nothing other than the material universe we can observe, concludes that there is no good and evil. Praise God, even those who claim such things do not live accordingly. For everyone knows deep down that good and evil do, in fact, exist, even if they do not recognize where this knowledge comes from.

Others say, "All we need is love" (defining love in an unbiblical way). Even granting their wrong understanding of true love, we could still ask: if the material universe is all there is, how can it be that the most important thing of all is an immaterial concept like love and that "blind, pitiless indifference" does not prevail?

The answer to all such claims is clear to those who trust in God's truth. Both a comprehensive plan and an ultimate purpose exist. Above all, it is indeed love that, at the deepest level, defines the universe since the whole universe flows from the eternal Triune love of the living God. *Instead of an epilogue,* then, because we need the truth of the greatest story to correctly understand our world and circumstances on a daily basis.

Finally, *instead of an epilogue* because this story does not leave us unaffected; we cannot say that we have learned it, and now we need not dwell on it any longer. On the contrary, *this story intends to incorporate our own personal stories into its narrative.* Indeed, God Himself calls us, through the greatest story, to the Son of His love and a life of conformity with the purpose for which He created us, namely, to manifest the glory of the grace of the LORD. *Let us too live, then, by Christ, with Christ, and for Christ.* Let us make it the highest purpose of our lives to continuously grow in His knowledge and make Him known to those around us. Let us live for the great commission. Let us lose our life for Christ and the Gospel to save it. Let us seek first the kingdom of God and His righteousness, trusting that all things necessary will be added to us. Let us continue in our pilgrimage until the day we see Him face to face and hear from His lips:

> *"Well done, good and faithful servant. You have been faithful over a little; I will set you over much. **Enter into the joy of your master**"* (Matt. 25:21, emphasis mine).

* * *

*Let everything that has breath
praise the LORD!
Praise the LORD!*

Psalm 150:6

Soli Deo Gloria!

APPENDIX

The awareness of Christ's Presence in the OT Scriptures in the works of older theologians

The unanimous testimony of the ancient Church was that the LORD Jesus Christ was really and physically Present throughout the OT era. The early Church recognized and proclaimed that the Angel LORD was the second Person of the Trinity, the God of the patriarchs and the prophets, who became incarnate in the fullness of time. As genuine successors of the early church, the sixteenth-century Reformers and their descendants recognized and proclaimed the same truth. *The quotations from the works of earlier theologians of various centuries, listed below, prove these assertions.*

The fact that such an important (and formerly widely held) truth has now largely been forgotten shows how necessary it is for each generation of Christians not to remain complacently contented with what they receive from the previous ones but, instead, to keep going back to the sources (Acts 17:11).

Justin Martyr [AD 100–165]

"Moses, then, the blessed and faithful servant of God, declares that He who appeared to Abraham under the oak in Mamre is God, sent with the two angels in His company to judge Sodom by Another who remains ever in the supercelestial places, invisible to all men, holding personal intercourse with none, whom we believe to be Maker and Father of all things; for he speaks thus: 'God appeared to him under the oak in Mamre, as he sat at his tent-door at noontide' [...] I shall attempt to persuade you, since you have understood the

163

Scriptures, [of the truth] of what I say, that there is, and that there is said to be, another God and Lord subject to the Maker of all things; who is also called an Angel, because He announces to men whatsoever the Maker of all things—above whom there is no other God—wishes to announce to them ... The Scripture just quoted by me will make this plain to you. It is thus: 'The sun was risen on the earth, and Lot entered into Segor (Zoar); and the Lord rained on Sodom sulfur and fire from the Lord out of heaven, and overthrew these cities and all the neighbourhood.'"

Dialogue with Trypho, a Jew, 56

"The Father of the universe has a Son; who also, being the first-begotten Word of God, is even God. And of old He [Christ] appeared in the shape of fire and in the likeness of an angel to Moses and to the other prophets; but now in the times of your reign, having, as we before said, become Man by a virgin, according to the counsel of the Father, for the salvation of those who believe on Him, He endured both to be set at nought and to suffer, that by dying and rising again He might conquer death. And that which was said out of the bush to Moses, 'I am that I am, the God of Abraham, and the God of Isaac, and the God of Jacob, and the God of your fathers,' this signified that they, even though dead, are let in existence, and are men belonging to Christ Himself."

First Apology, chapter 63

Irenaeus Of Lyons [c. AD 130–202]

"Wherefore also John does appropriately relate that the Lord said to the Jews: 'Ye search the Scriptures, in which ye think ye have eternal life; these are they which testify of me. And ye are not willing to come unto Me, that ye may have life.' How therefore did the Scriptures testify of Him, unless they were from one and the same

Father, instructing men beforehand as to the advent of His Son, and foretelling the salvation brought in by Him? 'For if ye had believed Moses, ye would also have believed Me; for he wrote of Me;' [saying this,] no doubt, because the Son of God is implanted everywhere throughout his writings: at one time, indeed, speaking with Abraham, when about to eat with him; at another time with Noah, giving to him the dimensions [of the ark]; at another inquiring after Adam; at another, bringing down judgment upon the Sodomites; and again, when He becomes visible, and directs Jacob on his journey, and speaks with Moses from the bush. And it would be endless to recount [the occasions] upon which the Son of God is shown forth by Moses. Of the day of His passion, too, he was not ignorant."

Against Heresies, Book IV (4.10.1)

"Since, therefore, the Father is truly Lord, and the Son truly Lord, the Holy Spirit has fitly designated them by the title of Lord. And again, referring to the destruction of the Sodomites, the Scripture says, 'Then the Lord rained upon Sodom and upon Gomorrah fire and brimstone from the Lord out of heaven.' For it here points out that the Son, who had also been talking with Abraham, had received power to judge the Sodomites for their wickedness."

Against Heresies, Book III (3.6.1)

Tertullian [AD 145–220]

"It is the Son, therefore, who has been from the beginning administering judgment, throwing down the haughty tower, and dividing the tongues, punishing the whole world by the violence of waters, raining upon Sodom and Gomorrah fire and brimstone, as the Lord from the Lord. For He it was who at all times came down to hold converse with men, from Adam on to the patriarchs and the prophets, in vision, in dream, in mirror, in dark saying; ever from the beginning laying the foundation of the course of His dispensations, which He meant to follow out to the very last. Thus was He ever learning even as God to converse with men upon earth, being no other than the Word which was to be made flesh. But He was thus learning (or rehearsing), in order to level for us the way of faith, that we might the more readily believe that the Son of God had come down into the world, if we knew that in times past also something similar had been done."

Treatise against Praxeas, 16

Cyprian [200–258]

Cyprian observes that "the Angel who appeared to the Patriarchs is Christ and God." And this he confirms by producing a number of those passages from the Old Testament where the Angel of the Lord appeared and spoke with the Patriarchs.

Treatise XII addressed to Quirinius,
Testimonies against the Jews, Book 2, sect. 5 & 6

Novatian [200–258]

"Therefore the Lord overturned Sodom, that is, God overturned Sodom; but in the overturning of Sodom, the Lord rained fire from the Lord. And this Lord was the God seen by Abraham; and this God was the guest of Abraham, certainly seen because He was also touched. But although the Father, being invisible, was assuredly not at that time seen, He who was accustomed to be touched and seen was seen and received to hospitality. But this [is] the Son of God, 'The Lord rained from the Lord upon Sodom and Gomorrah brimstone and fire.' And this is the Word of God. And the Word of God was made flesh, and dwelt among us; and this is Christ. It was not the Father, then, who was a guest with Abraham, but Christ. Nor was it the Father who was seen then, but the Son; and Christ was seen. Rightly, therefore, Christ is both Lord and God."

A Treatise of Novatian Concerning the Trinity, Chapter XVIII

Athanasius I of Alexandria (Athanasius the Great) [298–373]

"If then they suppose that the Saviour was not Lord and King, even before He became man and endured the Cross, but then began to be Lord, let them know that they are openly reviving the statements of the Samosatene. But if, as we have quoted and declared above, He is Lord and King everlasting, seeing that Abraham worships Him as Lord, and Moses says, 'Then the Lord rained upon Sodom and upon Gomorrah brimstone and fire from the Lord out of heaven;' and David in the Psalms, 'The Lord said unto my Lord, Sit on My right hand;' and, 'Your Throne, O God, is for ever and ever; a sceptre of righteousness is the sceptre of Your Kingdom;' and, 'Your Kingdom is an everlasting Kingdom;' it is plain that even before He became man, He was King and Lord everlasting, being Image and Word of the Father."

Second discourse against the Arians (2.15.13)

"But if it belong to none other than God to bless and to deliver, and none other was the deliverer of Jacob than the Lord himself and Him that delivered him the Patriarch besought for his grandsons, evidently none other did he join to God in his prayer [Gen. 48:15-16], than God's Word, whom therefore he called Angel, because it is He alone who reveals the Father."

Third discourse against the Arians (3.25.13)

Hilary of Poitiers [c. 310–367]

"The One who is called the Angel of God the same is Lord and God.

For the Son of God according to the Prophet is "the Angel of his great Council (or Covenant)" [LXX Isa. 9:6]. That the distinction of Persons might be entire He is called the Angel of God for he who is God of God the same also is the Angel or Messenger of God and yet that at the same time due honor might be paid to him he also is called Lord and God."

On the Trinity. Book 4, Ch. 23

Cyril [313–386]

Writing about Isaiah, where he saw God sitting upon the throne of his glory (Isa. 6), Cyril says, "The Father hath no man seen at any time but he who then appeared to the prophet was the Son."

The Catechetical Lectures of Cyril (14.27)

Basil [329–379]

"It is manifest to every one, that where the same Person is styled both an Angel and God, it must be meant of the only begotten, who manifested himself to mankind in different Generations, and declared the will of the Father to his Saints. Wherefore, He who at his appearing to Moses called himself, I AM, cannot be conceived to be any other person than God the Word, who was in the beginning with God."

Refutation Of Eunomius Apology II

Ambrose of Milan [340–397]

"It was not the Father Who spoke to Moses in the bush or in the desert, but the Son. It was of this Moses that Stephen said, 'This is he who was in the church, in the wilderness, with the Angel' [Acts vii.38]. This [the Son], then, is He Who gave the Law, Who spake with Moses saying, 'I am the God of Abraham, the God of Issaac, the God of Jacob.' This, then, is the God of the patriarchs, this is the God of the prophets."

Ambrose's Exposition of the Christian Faith. Book I.XIII

Jerome [347–420]

Jerome speaks of the unity of the sacred books. "Whatever," he asserts, "we read in the Old Testament we find also in the Gospel; and what we read in the Gospel is deduced from the Old Testament. There is no discord between them, no disagreement. In both Testaments the Trinity is preached."

Letter 18 to Pope Damascus

John Chrysostom [349–407]

"Now what is this one body? The faithful throughout the whole world, both which are, and which have been, and which shall be. And again, they that before Christ's coming pleased God, are "one body." How so? Because they also knew Christ. Whence does this appear? 'Your father Abraham,' saith He [Jesus], 'rejoiced to see My day, and he saw it, and was glad.' And again, 'If ye had believed Moses,' He saith, 'ye would have believed Me, for he wrote of Me.' And the prophets too would not have written of One, of whom they knew not what they said; whereas they both knew Him, and worshiped Him. Thus then were they also 'one body.'"

Homily X on Ephesians (Eph. 4:4)

Pope Leo I (Leo the Great) [400–461]

"[F]rom the constitution of the world He [God] ordained one and the same Cause of Salvation for all. For the grace of God, by which the whole body of the saints is ever justified, was augmented, not begun, when Christ was born."

On the Feast of the Nativity, III.4

Martin Luther [1483–1546]

"All the promises of God lead back to the first promise concerning Christ of Genesis 3:15. The faith of the fathers in the Old Testament era, and our faith in the New Testament are one and the same faith in Christ Jesus [...] The faith of the fathers was directed at the Christ who was to come, while ours rests in the Christ who has come. Time does not change the object of true faith, or the Holy Spirit. There has always been and always will be one mind, one impression, one faith concerning Christ among true believers whether they live in times past, now, or in times to come. We too believe in the Christ to come as the fathers did in the Old Testament, for we look for Christ to come again on the last day to judge the quick and the dead."

Luther's Commentary on Galatians 3:6-7

John Calvin [1509–1564]

Institutes of the Christian Religion:

"The god who of old appeared to the patriarchs was no other than Christ."

[Book 1, Chapter 13, Section 27 – 1.13.27]

"'No one sees the Father except the Son and anyone to whom the Son chooses to reveal Him' [Matt. 11:27b]—surely, they who would attain the knowledge of God should always be directed by that eternal Wisdom. For how could they either have comprehended God's mysteries with the mind, or have uttered them, except by the teaching of Him to whom alone the secrets of the Father are revealed? Therefore, holy men of old knew God only by beholding Him in His Son as in a mirror. When I say this, I mean that God has never manifested Himself to men in any other way than through the Son, that is, His sole wisdom, light and truth. From this fountain Adam, Noah, Abraham, Isaac, Jacob, and others drank all that they had of heavenly teaching. From the same fountain, all the prophets have also drawn every heavenly oracle that they have given forth."

[4.8.5]

"Faith in God is faith in Christ. God willed that the Jews should be so instructed by these prophecies that they might turn their eyes directly to Christ in order to seek deliverance [...] apart from Christ the saving knowledge of God does not stand. From the beginning of the world he had consequently been set before all the elect that they should look upon him and put their trust in him [...] God is comprehended in Christ alone [...] So today the Turks [Muslims], although they proclaim at the top of their lungs that the Creator of heaven and earth is God, still, while repudiating Christ, substitute an idol in place of the true God."

[2.6.4]

"The orthodox doctors of the church have correctly and wisely expounded, that the Word of God was the supreme angel, who then began, as it were with anticipation, to perform the office of Mediator. For though he were not clothed with flesh, yet he descended as in an intermediate form, that he might have more familiar access to the faithful. This closer intercourse procured for him the name of the angel; still, however, he retained the character which justly belonged to him, that of the God of ineffable glory."

[1.13.10]

John Owen [1616–1683]

"The glory of Christ was represented and made known under the Old Testament in his personal appearances to leaders of the church in their generations. In these appearances he was God only, but appeared in the assumed shape of a man to signify what he would one day actually be. He did not create a human nature and unite it to himself for a while. Rather, by his divine power he appeared in the shape of a man. In this way, Christ appeared to Abraham, to Jacob, to Moses, to Joshua and to others."

The Glory of Christ, Ch. 8

"He [the Word], by whom all things were made, and by whom all were to be renewed that were to be brought again unto God, did, in an especial and glorious manner, appear unto our first parents [Adam and Eve], as he in whom this whole dispensation centered, and unto whom it was committed. And as, after the promise given [Gen. 3:8], he appeared 'in human form', to instruct the Church in the mystery of his future incarnation, and under the name of Angel, to shadow out his office as sent unto it, and employed in it by the Father; so here, before the promise, he discovered his distinct glorious person, as the eternal Voice of the Father [Gen. 3:8]."

10th introductory essay: Appearances of the Son of God under the Old Testament (Commentary on Hebrews, vol. 1)

Blaise Pascal [1623–1662]

"Moses first teaches the Trinity, original sin, the Messiah."

Pensées, 751

Jonathan Edwards [1703–1758]

"And therefore, when we read in sacred history what God did from time to time towards his Church and people, and what he said to them, and how he revealed Himself to them, we are to understand it especially of the second person of the Trinity. When we read of God's appearing after the fall, from time to time in some visible form or outward symbol of his presence, we are ordinarily, if not universally, to understand it of the second person of the Trinity; which may be argued from John I. 18: "No man hath seen God at any time; the only begotten Son, which is in the bosom of the Father, he hath declared him." He [the Son] is therefore called "the image of the invisible God," Col. I. 15; intimating that though God the Father be invisible, yet Christ is his image or representation, by which he [the Father] is seen, or by which the Church of God hath often had a representation of him, that is not invisible, and in particular that Christ has after appeared in a human form."

A History of the Work of Redemption, Part I.I

Charles Spurgeon [1834–1892]

"Ver. 7. The angel of the Lord. The covenant angel, the Lord Jesus, at the head of all the bands of heaven, surrounds with his army the dwellings of the saints. Like hosts entrenched so are the ministering spirits encamped around the Lord's chosen, to serve and succour, to defend and console them. Encampeth round about them that fear him. On every side the watch is kept by warriors of sleepless eyes, and the Captain of the host is one whose prowess none can resist. And delivereth them. We little know how many providential deliverances we owe to those unseen hands which are charged to bear us up lest we dash our foot against a stone."

The Treasury of David, comments on Psalm 34:7

Anthony Tyrrell Hanson [1916–1991]

"One element in NT exegesis …, rather than typology as such, is the most important clue to the understanding of the NT exegesis of the OT. That element may be called the real presence of the pre-existent Christ in OT history—or, to be more accurate, the real presence of the pre-existent Jesus. 'Jesus in the Old Testament' is, in fact, the way in which the NT writers for the most part thought of it … The normative approach of the NT writers to the OT is not that of typology but rather that of what we have called 'real presence.'"

Jesus Christ in the Old Testament (London: SPCK, 1965), 7-8
(Quoted in Matt Foreman, "Real Presence in the Old Testament." Reformation21, March 16, 2022. https://www.reformation21.org/blog/real-presence-in-the-old-testament)

SUGGESTIONS FOR FURTHER READING

Athanasius of Alexandria. "The Letter to Marcellinus on the Interpretation of the Psalms" https://www.semperreformanda.com/psalmody/a-letter-of-athanasius-on-the-interpretation-of-the-psalms/.

Batzig, Nicholas T. (22/5/2013). "The Songs of the Son (Seeing Christ in the Psalms)" http://feedingonchrist.org/the-songs-of-the-son-seeing-christ-in-the-psalms/.

Batzig, Nicholas T. (25/6/2015). "Eternalizing the Old Testament" http://www.alliancenet.org/christward/eternalizing-the-old-testament.

Batzig, Nicholas T. (14/1/2014). "Death and Resurrection: the Key to the Old Testament" http://www.alliancenet.org/christward/death-and-resurrection-the-key-to-the-old-testament.

Binnie, William. *A Pathway into the Psalter: The Psalms, Their History, Teachings and Use.* Solid Ground Christian Books, 2005.

Blackham, Paul. (23/3/2001). "Faith in Christ in the Old Testament" http://www.theologian.org.uk/bible/blackham.html.

Borland, James A. *Christ in the Old Testament – Old Testament appearances of Christ in Human Form.* Christian Focus Publications, 2010.

Boyarin, Daniel. "The Gospel of the Memra: Jewish Binitarianism and the Prologue to John". The Harvard Theological Review, Vol. 94, No. 3 (Jul. 2001): 243–284 https://www.researchgate.net/publication/231982610_The_Gospel_of_the_Memra_Jewish_Binitarianism_and_the_prologue_to_John.

Carden, Travis. "Total Depravity Verse List" http://traviscarden.com/total-depravity-verse-list.

Cho, Dongsun. "Justification in Marius Victorinus' Pauline Commentaries: Sola Fide, Solo Christo, and Sola Gratia Dei". Journal for Baptist Theology & Ministry 11:1 (2014): 3–25 https://www.nobts.edu/baptist-center-theology/journals/journals/JBTM_11-1_Spring_2014.pdf#page=6.

Clowney, Edmund P. "The Singing Savior". Moody Monthly (July-August 1979): 40–42 https://15degreessouth.files.wordpress.com/2014/08/clowney_jxsings.pdf.

Edwards, Jonathan. *A History of the Work of Redemption.* 1773. https://www.monergism.com/history-work-redemption-ebook.

Fentiman, Travis. "Do We Sing Jesus Christ's Name in the Psalter?" https://reformedbooksonline.com/do-we-sing-jesus-name-in-the-psalms/.

Fesko, John V. *Justification: Understanding the Classic Reformed Doctrine.* P & R Publishing, 2008.

Garner, David B. (11/9/2014). "The Jesus of the Old and New" http://www.alliancenet.org/placefortruth/column/sine-qua-non/the-jesus-of-the-old-and-new.

Gieschen, Charles A. "The Real Presence of the Son Before Christ: Revisiting an Old Approach to Old Testament Christology". Concordia Theological Quarterly 68:2 (April 2004): 105–126 http://www.ctsfw.net/media/pdfs/gieschenrealpresence.pdf.

Gill, John. *Exposition of the Entire Bible.* 18th century. http://biblehub.com/commentaries/gill/.

Hamilton, James M. Jr. "The Messianic Music of the Song of Songs: A Non-Allegorical Interpretation". WTJ 68 (2006): 331–345.

Hanson, Anthony T. *Jesus Christ in the Old Testament.* SPCK, 1965.

Heiser, Michael. "The Jewish Trinity: How the Old Testament Reveals the Christian Godhead" http://misclane.blogspot.gr/2013/06/the-jewish-trinity-how-old-testament.html.

Heiser, Michael. "Two Powers in Heaven" https://drmsh.com/the-naked-bible/two-powers-in-heaven/.

Heiser, Michael. "Trinitarian Jewish Thinking Before Jesus" http://drmsh.com/trinitarian-jewish-thinking-before-jesus/.

Hoekema, Anthony A. *Saved by Grace.* Williams B. Eerdmans Publishing Company, 1989.

Hoekema, Anthony A. *The Bible and the Future.* Grand Rapids: Eerdmans, 1979.

Hoekema, Anthony A. *Created in God's Image.* Grand Rapids: Eerdmans, 1986.

Juncker, Günther. "Christ As Angel: The Reclamation Of A Primitive Title". Trinity Journal 15:2 (Fall 1994): 221–250 http://earlychurch.org.uk/pdf/angel_juncker.pdf.

Keach, Benjamin. *Tropologia: A Key to Open Scripture Metaphors.* William Hill Collingridge, 1858.

Levy, Steve. Blackham, Paul. *Bible Overview.* Christian Focus, 2008.

Luther, Martin. *The Bondage of the Will* (1525 AD), translated by J.I. Packer and O.R. Johnston. Grand Rapids: Revel, 1996.

Luther, Martin. *On the last words of David* (1543 AD), translated by H. Cole, Select Works of Martin Luther, vol. II. 1826.

Macleod, Donald. *The Person of Christ.* Inter Varsity Press, 1998.

McGrath, James F. and Jerry Truex. "'Two Powers' and Early Jewish and Christian Monotheism". Journal of Biblical Studies 4.1 (2004): 43-71 https://works.bepress.com/jamesmcgrath/36/.

Metzger, Paul Louis (Editor). *Trinitarian Soundings in Systematic Theology.* T & T Clark International, 2005.

Moody, Andrew. "That All May Honour the Son: Holding Out for a Deeper Christocentrism". Themelios 36.3 (2011), 403–14 https://www.thegospelcoalition.org/themelios/article/that-all-may-honour-the-son-holding-out-for-a-deeper-christocentrism/.

Murray, David. *Jesus on every page.* Thomas Nelson, 2013.

Murray, John. *Redemption Accomplished and Applied.* Williams B. Eerdmans Publishing Company, 1955.

Owen, John. *The Glory of Christ.* The Banner of Truth Trust, 1994.

Owen, John. *Communion with God.* The Banner of Truth Trust, 1991.

Packer, James I. *Knowing God.* Downers Grove, Ill. InterVarsity Press, 1973.

Pelt, Miles Van. "Gospel-Centered Hermeneutics: Foundations and Principles of Evangelical and Biblical Interpretation" https://www.reformation21.org/articles/gospelcentered-hermeneutics-foundations-and-principles-of-evangelical-and-biblic-1.php.

Pitchford, Nathan. "The Reformers' Hermeneutic: Grammatical, Historical, and Christ-Centered" https://www.uniontheology.org/resources/life/pastoral/the-reformers-hermeneutic-grammatical-historical-and-christ-centred.

Reeves, Michael. *The Good God. Enjoying Father, Son and Spirit.* Paternoster, 2012.

Sailhamer, John. "The Messiah and the Hebrew Bible". Journal of the Evangelical Theological Society 44 (2001): 5–23 https://www.etsjets.org/files/JETS-PDFs/44/44-1/44-1-PP005-024_JETS.pdf.

Saville, Andy. "Paul Blackham: a Trinitarian Reading of the Old Testament" https://biblicalstudies.org.uk/pdf/churchman/123-04_341.pdf.

Scrivener, Glen. "Christ in the Old Testament" http://christthetruth.net/christ-in-ot/.

Segal, Alan F. *Two Powers in Heaven. Early Rabbinic Reports about Christianity and Gnosticism.* SJLA 25. Leiden: E. J. Brill, 1977.

Shamoun, Sam. "An Examination of God's Uniplurality in light of the Hebrew Bible's Use of Plurals" http://www.answering-islam.org/Shamoun/plurality1.htm.

Spurgeon, C. H. *The Treasury of David* (1885). Abridged by David O. Fuller. Kregel Publications, 1976.

Spurgeon, C. H. *Christ's Glorious Achievements – Set Forth in 7 Sermons.* UK, 1877.

Stott, John R. W. *The Cross of Christ.* Inter-Varsity Press, 2006.

Van Dorn, Douglas. *Christ in the Old Testament – From the Shadows to the Savior.* Waters of Creation Publishing, 2015.

Van Dorn, Douglas. "Christ: The Word of God" https://thedecablog.wordpress.com/2014/08/23/christ-in-the-old-testament-part-vi-cont/.

Walvoord, John F. "Series in Christology–Part 2: The Preincarnate Son of God". Bibliotheca Sacra 104:414 (1947): 154–169 http://walvoord.com/series/336.

HEIDELBERG CATECHISM REVISED ACCORDING TO THE ORIGINALS, Traditional Language Version, 2014 Edition, RCUS (The Reformed Church in the United States), available at: https://rcus.org/wp-content/uploads/2021/12/Heidelberg-Catechism-Traditional.pdf.

ENDNOTES

1   Iésous – Jesus, the transliteration of the Hebrew name Yehoshua/Jehoshua (contracted to "Joshua") which means "YHWH saves" (or "YHWH is salvation"). "YHWH" is the proper name of God in the original Hebrew.

God's name is composed of four Hebrew consonants: YHWH, known as the tetragrammaton (meaning "four letters"). Because of the lack of vowels, Bible scholars debate how the tetragrammaton *YHWH* was pronounced. The most likely choice for how the tetragrammaton was pronounced is *Yahweh.*

Thayer, Joseph H. *A Greek-English Lexicon of the New Testament* (1889), 300
Strong's Concordance, 2424. Iésous – http://biblehub.com/greek/2424.htm
Strong's Concordance, 3091. Yehoshua – https://biblehub.com/hebrew/3091.htm
Britannica, T. Editors of Encyclopedia. "Yahweh." *Encyclopedia Britannica,* January 2, 2023. https://www.britannica.com/topic/Yahweh

2   For a more expanded treatment of the NT's handling of the OT concerning the person and work of Christ, see these blog posts by Glen Scrivener:
https://www.christthetruth.net/2008/05/12/christ-in-the-old-testament-12/
https://www.christthetruth.net/2008/05/14/christ-in-the-old-testament-13/

3   The English word *gospel* comes from old English *gōdspel* (gōd 'good' + spel 'news'), which is a translation of late Latin *evangelium,* which is a transliteration from ancient Greek *euangelion,* which, of course, means Good News! *Merriam-Webster.com Dictionary,* s.v. "gospel," accessed April 17, 2023, https://www.merriam-webster.com/dictionary/gospel

4   Quoted in Charles A. Gieschen, "The Real Presence of the Son Before Christ: Revisiting an Old Approach to Old Testament Christology". Concordia Theological Quarterly 68:2 (April 2004), 108

5   Henry Morris. *Men of Science, Men of God* (Master Books, 1988), 21

6   Edited by Nancy K. Frankenberry. *The Faith of Scientists: In Their Own Words* (Princeton University Press, 2008), 45

7   As quoted in Dimitrov Tihomir's free eBook: *50 Nobel Laureates and Other Great Scientists Who Believe in God,* (2008), 101, available at: http://nobelists.net, last accessed in 20/6/2016.

8   The interested reader is encouraged to study the vast number of many Christian scientists' quotations contained in the books mentioned in the previous three footnotes.

9   I am grateful to Travis Carden for his immensely helpful categorization of the Bible verses that explain the extent and magnitude of the Fall of humanity.

Travis Carden. "Total Depravity Verse List", January 9, 2007, http://traviscarden.com/total-depravity-verse-list

10   Roman Catholicism's false traditions concerning man's free will were opposed by Martin Luther and the entire religious reformation of the sixteenth century. Luther wrote in 1525 AD: "Hence it follows that 'free-will' without God's grace is not free at all, but is the permanent prisoner and bond slave of evil, since it cannot turn itself to good [p. 104] ... 'free-will' is a nonentity, *a thing* (I have used that word) *consisting of a name alone* [p. 271]." Martin Luther. *The Bondage of the Will*, tr. by J.I. Packer and O.R. Johnston, (Grand Rapids, MI: Revell, 1994)

11   HEIDELBERG CATECHISM REVISED ACCORDING TO THE ORIGINALS, Traditional Language Version, 2014 Edition, RCUS (The Reformed Church in the United States), available at: https://rcus.org/wp-content/uploads/2021/12/Heidelberg-Catechism-Traditional.pdf

12   For further references to the Angel of the Lord see: Genesis 16:9-14, 21:17-20, 22:11-18, 31:11-13, 48:15-16; Exodus 3:1-15, 13:21 <=> 14:19, 23:20-23, 32:34, 33:2 <=> 34:9; Numbers 20:16, 22:22-35; Judges 2:1-5, 6:11-24, 13:3-23; 2 Samuel 24:16-17; 1 Kings 19:5, 7; 2 Kings 1:3, 15; 1 Chronicles 21:11-20; Psalms 34:7-9, 35:5-6; Isaiah 63:9 <=> Exodus 33:14; Daniel 3:24-28, 6:22-23; Hosea 12:4-5 <=> Genesis 32:24-30; Zechariah 1:8-19, 3:1-10; Malachi 3:1. The many OT references to the Angel of the Lord (Malak Yahweh) indicate the *principal* importance of this Person.

For a thorough exploration of the OT's Christophanies see: Anthony Rogers, The Malak Yahweh: Jesus, the Divine Messenger of the Old Testament. Available at: https://www.answering-islam.org/authors/rogers/malak_yahweh1.html

Finally, Thomas Coke, in his commentary on Hosea 12:5, made the astonishing proposition that, on grammatical grounds, the translation of the Hebrew phrase "Malak Yahweh" should best be rendered as *"Jehovah-Angel", rather than "Angel of the Lord"*:

The holy prophet first calls him *angel,* מלאך, *malaak,* Hosea 12:4 and after mention of the wrestling or colluctation, and of the meeting and conference at

Beth-el, says, (Hosea 12:5.) that he, whom he had called *angel,* was JEHOVAH *God of Hosts.* And to make the assertion of this person's godhead, if possible, still more unequivocal, he adds, that to him belonged, as his appropriate memorial, that name, which is declarative of the very essence of the godhead. This *Man* therefore of the book of Genesis, this *Angel* of Hosea, who wrestled with Jacob, could be no other than the JEHOVAH-ANGEL, of whom we so often read in the English Bible, under the name of the *Angel of the Lord:* a phrase of an unfortunate structure, and so ill-conformed to the original, that it is to be feared, it has led many into the error of conceiving of the Lord as one person, and of the Angel as another. The word of the Hebrew, ill rendered, *the Lord,* is not, like the English word, an appellative, expressing rank, or condition; but it is the proper name JEHOVAH. And this proper name Jehovah is not, in the Hebrew, a genitive after the noun substantive *Angel,* as the English represents it; but the words *Jehovah* and *Angel,* are two nouns substantive in apposition, both speaking of the same person; the one, by the appropriate name of the essence; the other, by a title of office. *Jehovah-Angel* would be a better rendering. The JEHOVAH-ANGEL of the Old Testament is no other than He, who, in the fullness of time, "was incarnate by the Holy Ghost of the Virgin Mary."

Thomas Coke. "Commentary on Hosea 12:5". *Thomas Coke's Commentary on the Holy Bible* (1801-1803). Available at: www.studylight.org/commentaries/tcc/hosea-12.html

13 This translation is called Septuagint or LXX, (meaning "seventy") because, according to Jewish tradition, seventy-two translators worked to complete the translation of the Hebrew Bible into Greek around the third century BC (seventy-two is rounded down to seventy, hence the Roman numeral LXX).

14 E.g., the ESV preface states: "As is common among English translations today, the ESV usually renders the personal name of God (YHWH) with the word "LORD" (printed in small capitals)."

15 D. A. Carson. "The Ground of All Human Assurance Before God." The Gospel Coalition, January 27, 2016. https://www.thegospelcoalition.org/article/the-ground-of-all-human-assurance-before-god/

16 Steve Levy also expresses the same understanding concerning the presence of two distinct Divine Persons on Mount Sinai and their communication with Moses. In a section titled "The triune God meets Moses," he states that "Jesus meets Moses" (citing Exod. 33:11) and that "The Father meets Moses through Jesus" (citing Exod. 33:20-23 and 1 Cor. 10:4). See Steve Levy, Paul Blackham. *Bible Overview* (Christian Focus, 2008), 119

17 In the Hebrew Bible, the section of prophetic books included the following books: Joshua, Judges, Samuel (I and II), Kings (I and II), Jeremiah, Ezekiel, Isaiah, and the twelve minor Prophets. The historical books of this group were called the 'first Prophets.' They were thus named because they recorded the fulfillment of the prophecy of Moses. At the end of the Pentateuch (Deut. 31:14-29) Moses prophesied that the people would deny the LORD and violate His commandments, and, as a result, would be exiled from the promised land. Indeed, this is what happened after a few centuries.

18 Josephus Flavius, *Antiquities of the Jews.* Book XI, chapter 1, para. 1 & 2
Josephus Flavius, Antiquities of the Jews. Book XI, chapter 1, para. 1 & 2

19 Isaiah's prophecy was written more than seven hundred years before the incarnation of the LORD Jesus. The 53rd chapter clearly portrays His mission, and it clearly displays the Messiah dying for the sins of His people and then returning back to life. Such is its detail that some have tried to ignore it by claiming that it was written by Jesus' disciples *after* His crucifixion. However, in 1947 AD, in the caves of Qumran, various manuscripts in the Hebrew language were found. Among them, the "Great Isaiah Scroll" was discovered. This scroll contains the entire book of Isaiah and is dated around 150 to 100 BC! That is, before the incarnation. For more details see: https://en.wikipedia.org/wiki/Isaiah_Scroll

20 Westminster Larger Catechism, OPC (The Orthodox Presbyterian Church). Available at: https://opc.org/documents/LCLayout.pdf

21 The third and last section of the Hebrew Bible includes the following books: Psalms, Proverbs, Job, Ecclesiastes, Song of Songs, Ruth, Lamentations, Daniel, Esther, Ezra, Nehemiah, and Chronicles.

22 I am grateful to David Murray for this categorization. David Murray. *Jesus on every page* (Thomas Nelson, 2013), 187—88

23 C. H. Spurgeon. *The Treasury of David* (1885). Abridged by David O. Fuller (Kregel Publications, 1976), 213

24 C. H. Spurgeon. *The Treasury of David,* 99

25 William Binnie. *The Psalms: Their History, Teachings and Use* (1870), 189

26 John Gill. *Exposition of the Entire Bible,* Psalm 16

27 Quoted in: Andrew A. Bonar. *Christ and His Church in the Book of Psalms* (1860), ix

28 Quoted in: David Murray. *Jesus on every page* (Thomas Nelson, 2013), 196—97

29 These are indeed the documented historical events, in spite of various deliberate

attempts to falsify the truth, such as *The Da Vinci Code* novel. To prove the historical veracity of Christianity's central claims, two testimonies of non-Christian Roman citizens will be cited. One was a historian, the other a magistrate:

1) *Cornelius Tacitus* (56-120 AD) in his description (Annals) of what happened on 64 AD during the great fire in Rome mentions that *Christ was crucified at the hands of Pontius Pilate* and that Christians then present in Rome were persecuted for their faith in Christ.

2) *Pliny the Younger* (61-113 AD) in one of his letters to the emperor in 112 AD mentions that *Christians met regularly to worship Jesus as God,* and that the first Christians upheld a high moral code.

For more details see: https://coldcasechristianity.com/writings/is-there-any-evidence-for-jesus-outside-the-bible/

30 Marius Victorinus lived during the fourth century AD. He was a Roman scholar who converted to Christianity at a relatively advanced age. Among his extant works are multiple commentaries on various letters of the apostle Paul. He was one of the first Christian theologians (if not the first, particularly in the Latin language) to produce such comprehensive commentaries on Paul's writings.

31 Stephen Andrew Cooper. *Marius Victorinus' Commentary on Galatians* (Oxford University Press, 2005), 332

32 HEIDELBERG CATECHISM REVISED ACCORDING TO THE ORIGINALS

33 Jonathan Gibson. "10 things you should know about definite atonement." Crossway, September 05, 2016. https://www.crossway.org/articles/10-things-you-should-know-about-definite-atonement/ (Last accessed: October 21, 2022)

34 HEIDELBERG CATECHISM REVISED ACCORDING TO THE ORIGINALS

35 Richard Dawkins. *River Out of Eden: A Darwinian View of Life* (Basic Books, 1996), 133

www.ingramcontent.com/pod-product-compliance
Lightning Source LLC
Chambersburg PA
CBHW041626140626
46547CB00030B/1084